# 9/11 and Collective Memory
# in US Classrooms

While current literature stresses the importance of teaching about the 9/11 attacks on the US, many questions remain as to what teachers are actually teaching in their own classrooms. Few studies address how teachers are using of all of this advice and curriculum, what sorts of activities they are undertaking, and how they go about deciding what they will do. Arguing that the events of 9/11 have become a "chosen trauma" for the US, author Cheryl Duckworth investigates how 9/11 is being taught in classrooms (if at all) and what narrative is being passed on to today's students about that day.

Using quantitative and qualitative data gathered from US middle and high school teachers, this volume reflects on foreign policy developments and trends since September 11th, 2001 and analyzes what this might suggest for future trends in U.S. foreign policy. The understanding that the "post-9/11 generation" has of what happened and what it means is significant to how Americans will view foreign policy in the coming decades (especially in the Islamic World) and whether it is likely to generate war or foster peace.

**Cheryl Lynn Duckworth**, Ph.D., is a professor of conflict resolution at Nova Southeastern University, USA, whose teaching and research focus on transforming the social, cultural, political and economic causes of war and violence. She regularly lectures and presents workshops on peace education, conflict resolution and historical memory. Among her recent publications is *Conflict Resolution and the Scholarship of Engagement*.

# Routledge Research in Education

*For a full list of titles in this series, please visit www.routledge.com.*

95 **The Resegregation of Schools**
Education and Race in the
Twenty-First Century
*Edited by Jamel K. Donnor
and Adrienne D. Dixson*

96 **Autobiographical Writing and
Identity in EFL Education**
*Shizhou Yang*

97 **Online Learning and
Community Cohesion**
Linking Schools
*Roger Austin and Bill Hunter*

98 **Language Teachers and
Teaching**
Global Perspectives, Local
Initiatives
*Edited by Selim Ben Said
and Lawrence Jun Zhang*

99 **Towards Methodologically
Inclusive Research Syntheses**
Expanding Possibilities
*Harsh Suri*

100 **Raising Literacy Achievement
in High-Poverty Schools**
An Evidence-Based Approach
*Eithne Kennedy*

101 **Learning and Collective
Creativity**
Activity-Theoretical and
Sociocultural Studies
*Annalisa Sannino and Viv Ellis*

102 **Educational Inequalities**
Difference and Diversity in
Schools and Higher Education
*Edited by Kalwant Bhopal
and Uvanney Maylor*

103 **Education, Social Background
and Cognitive Ability**
The Decline of the Social
*Gary N. Marks*

104 **Education in Computer
Generated Environments**
*Sara de Freitas*

105 **The Social Construction of
Meaning**
Reading Literature in Urban
English Classrooms
*John Yandell*

106 **Global Perspectives on
Spirituality in Education**
*Edited by Jacqueline Watson,
Marian de Souza
and Ann Trousdale*

107 **Neo-liberal Educational Reforms**
A Critical Analysis
*Edited by David A. Turner
and Hüseyin Yolcu*

108 **The Politics of Pleasure in
Sexuality Education**
Pleasure Bound
*Edited by Louisa Allen, Mary
Lou Rasmussen, and Kathleen
Quinlivan*

109 **Popular Culture, Pedagogy and Teacher Education**
International Perspectives
*Edited by Phil Benson and Alice Chik*

110 **Teacher Training and the Education of Black Children**
Bringing Color into Difference
*Uvanney Maylor*

111 **Secrecy and Tradecraft in Educational Administration**
The Covert Side of Educational Life
*Eugenie A. Samier*

112 **Affirming Language Diversity in Schools and Society**
Beyond Linguistic Apartheid
*Edited by Pierre Wilbert Orelus*

113 **Teacher Leadership**
New Conceptions for Autonomous Student Learning in the Age of the Internet
*Kokila Roy Katyal and Colin Evers*

114 **Test Fraud**
Statistical Detection and Methodology
*Edited by Neal M. Kingston and Amy K. Clark*

115 **Literacy, Play and Globalization**
Converging Imaginaries in Children's Critical and Cultural Performances
*Carmen Liliana Medina and Karen E. Wohlwend*

116 **Biotechnology, Education and Life Politics**
Debating Genetic Futures from School to Society
*Pádraig Murphy*

117 **Vernaculars in the Classroom**
Paradoxes, Pedagogy, Possibilities
*Shondel Nero and Dohra Ahmad*

118 **Professional Uncertainty, Knowledge and Relationship in the Classroom**
A Psycho-social Perspective
*Joseph Mintz*

119 **Negotiating Privilege and Identity in Educational Contexts**
*Adam Howard, Aimee Polimeno, and Brianne Wheeler*

120 **Liberty and Education**
A Civic Republican Approach
*Geoffrey Hinchliffe*

121 **Constructing Narratives of Continuity and Change**
A Transdisciplinary Approach to Researching Lives
*Edited by Hazel Reid and Linden West*

122 **Education, Philosophy and Wellbeing**
New Perspectives on the Work of John White
*Edited by Judith Suissa, Carrie Winstanley and Roger Marples*

123 **Chinese Students' Writing in English**
Implications from a Corpus-driven Study
*Maria Leedham*

124 **9/11 and Collective Memory in US Classrooms**
Teaching about Terror
*Cheryl Lynn Duckworth*

# 9/11 and Collective Memory in US Classrooms
Teaching About Terror

Cheryl Lynn Duckworth

NEW YORK   LONDON

First published 2015
by Routledge
711 Third Avenue, New York, NY 10017

and by Routledge
2 Park Square, Milton Park, Abingdon, Oxon OX14 4RN

*Routledge is an imprint of the Taylor & Francis Group,*
*an informa business*

© 2015 Taylor & Francis

The right of Cheryl Lynn Duckworth to be identified as author of this
work has been asserted by her in accordance with sections 77 and 78 of
the Copyright, Designs and Patents Act 1988.

All rights reserved. No part of this book may be reprinted or reproduced or
utilised in any form or by any electronic, mechanical, or other means, now
known or hereafter invented, including photocopying and recording, or in
any information storage or retrieval system, without permission in writing
from the publishers.

**Trademark Notice:** Product or corporate names may be trademarks or
registered trademarks, and are used only for identification and explanation
without intent to infringe.

*Library of Congress Cataloging-in-Publication Data*
A catalog record has been requested for this book.

ISBN13: 978-0-415-74201-6 (hbk)
ISBN13: 978-1-315-81492-6 (ebk)

Typeset in Sabon
by IBT Global.

# Contents

| | | |
|---|---|---|
| *List of Figures* | | ix |
| *Acknowledgments* | | xi |
| 1 | Classrooms, and a Country, Cope | 1 |
| 2 | Peace Education, Chosen Trauma and Collective Memory in the Classroom | 29 |
| 3 | Inside the Classroom | 47 |
| 4 | Educator Narratives of Teaching Terror | 60 |
| 5 | School Culture and the Power of Neoliberalism | 97 |
| 6 | Teaching 9/11 as an Opportunity for Narrative Transformation | 108 |
| *Appendix A: Survey of Teachers* | | 121 |
| *Appendix B: Interview Guide* | | 125 |
| *References* | | 127 |
| *Index* | | 133 |

# Figures and Charts

**FIGURES**

Figure 2.1    Model: Lederach 2005, p. 141.                              35

**CHARTS**

Chart 1                                                                          48
Chart 9                                                                          49
Chart 4                                                                          50
Chart 6                                                                          51
Chart 5                                                                          52
Chart 8                                                                          53
Chart 2                                                                          56

# Acknowledgements

I owe thanks to so many for supporting the completion of this book. First and foremost, my thanks to my Chair, Michele Rice and my Dean, Honggang Yang, for the support of a Research and Development term. My thanks to supportive colleagues who helped me disseminate my survey.

Many thanks to my hardworking Graduate Assistants, Naupess Kibiswa, Sharon McIntyre, and Aleks Nesic, for your research and survey number-crunching skills. Ideas marinate in relationships and over time, so I would also like to thank the brilliant students in my 2012 graduate seminar, "History, Memory and Conflict Resolution". Your ideas and our rich dialogues echo in these pages. Thank you as well to discussants, chairs and participants at numerous conferences with insightful feedback and encouragement. Thanks especially to my dear colleague, Richard Rubenstein, for early comments on the draft and a special thanks to Ayaz Naseem for his warm encouragement of this project. Most importantly of all, my profound and sincere thanks to each and every teacher who took the time to respond to my survey and call for interviews. I've been there and I know of the demands on your time, emotions and mental energy. Your shared your time generously and inspired me with your compassion and creativity. I hope I have told your story well in this book!

Finally, I'd like to thank Eddie, Mom, Dad, Paula, Rebecca, Peter and Jack—for love, support and listening, without which I could not have sustained such a project. I love you!

# 1 Classrooms, and a Country, Cope

## THE MOURNING AFTER

One of the most common questions a citizen might ask another citizen when reflecting on some shared collective grief or trauma is, "Where were you then?" Given that this work is an exploration of the role of historical memory with regards to how we tell ourselves the story of what happened on 9/11—and therefore what we tell our students—it seems appropriate to begin with a brief reflection on where I myself was that ironically gorgeous September morning. On the morning of September 11, 2001, I was standing in front of my freshman English high school classroom in Fredericksburg, VA. As students filed in for the beginning of second period, one student—the class clown, strangely enough—told me I needed to turn on the TV.

I laughed, ignoring his advice and welcoming him to class.

He repeated himself: "You should turn on the TV. Something's happened."

In 2001 we were well into the cell phone age, and a couple of other students were already receiving calls from friends and family. (Our school was not too far south from Arlington, VA, and many of our students had parents working at Langley or the Pentagon.) Soon an announcement came over the PA system. I turned on the TV to CNN and watched the Twin Towers burn and crumble with twenty or so fourteen-year-olds. We dismissed early that day, and I drove home knowing everything had changed. I can recall phoning my father (who served in the Army twenty-six years) and asking him if World War III had started. He said yes, he believed so. Later that week, our school had an emergency staff meeting centered on taking care of ourselves and coping with any trauma our students might be experiencing. The meeting began with the facilitator asking us how we ourselves were doing, a kindness which I still remember. As it happened, at least one of our students lost her father (who worked at the Pentagon). She withdrew from school and her family moved away, presumably to try to start over.

Like many of us, what I recall most vividly over ten years later is that infamous image of the planes themselves, having been turned into a missile, crashing into the Towers. What I admit to be an overdose of media

## 2   9/11 and Collective Memory in U.S. Classrooms

coverage on my part, seared into my mind the picture of the smoke and flames and the gaping hole in the Trade Center, against a vivid blue sky. For me the most horrific detail was the realization that the small black ovals falling from the Towers were people who had jumped. I took the following couple of days of class to open the classroom floor up for sharing of any thoughts or feelings my students (high school freshman and sophomores in English) might have. Like most of us, they expressed fear, pain, shock and confusion. They wondered what it might mean for the future. One student in 7th period—I can still see her short strawberry blonde hair and freckles, though I admit I can't remember her name—brought me a set of pictures she had printed out from the Web; they were images of vigils that had been held worldwide in the aftermath of the attacks. One was of the late Yasser Arafat donating blood; I wondered: did she know who he was? Did she understand the political or historical significance of someone including his picture? She mentioned to me that she brought them since I was apparently the only teacher who had discussed the attacks in the classroom. Wanting to counter the idea the U.S. was globally hated, a misimpression many of my students harbored, I posted a few of the vigil pictures up on the bulletin board.

In the days immediately following, I can remember crying at random and unexpected moments, driving home from work or running errands. I will forever associate the U2 ballad "Peace on Earth" with the events of 9/11, as my local radio station played it incessantly in the weeks following the attacks. Neighbors and strangers seemed unusually patient and kind, greeting one another in line at gas stations and grocery stores. I found myself ending each conversation with family by saying, "I love you". Grieving as so many were in the raw days afterword, I sat with several friends glued to CNN. Needing to express the sadness and rage, I wrote the below poem and have often shared it with students on the memorial date of 9/11.

> The sky is falling—Ashes, Armageddon,
> Clouds of metal rain.
>
> Six hundred miles south in safety,
> how dare the sun shine?
> The breeze is mild and warm
> as I thunder inside,
> the only lightning within my chest,
> the only rain pours down my cheeks,
> while my fists shake like crumblingtowers.

It joins thousands of other news articles, photos, keepsakes, letters, saved cell phone messages, poems and media footage as a real-time documentation of what occurred. Together these represent the raw material for the collective narrative that is still being shaped about the meaning of 9/11

*Classrooms, and a Country, Cope* 3

and its impact. Have we, as a nation, now processed it and recovered, and moved on? Did 9/11 in fact fundamentally reshape how Americans understand ourselves (themselves) or has there been some sort of return to normal? How will today's middle and high school students view 9/11 and by extension "the Islamic World"? (Because this phrase, if we really reflect on it, can refer to countries as dramatically different as Albania, Indonesia and Lebanon, I dislike it. Hence the quotes. That said, it is commonly used and so I adopt it for convenience.) Will they indeed associate the two or will they (one prays) have been educated into a more contextualized, historically grounded and nuanced view of the relationship been the U.S. and the world's Muslims? A core reason for this book, of course, is to ask and contribute to the answers to these urgent questions.

For me 9/11 was how best to respond as an educator and a global citizen. I found myself saving the newspapers from the days immediately subsequent. My stint in Zimbabwe as Peace Corps volunteer was suddenly, unpredictably salient. The need to reconnect with the global community, as I had experienced it many times as an expatriate, was fierce. I am certain that this is a large part of why I decided to ultimately leave teaching English and pursue international peace and conflict studies. Perhaps it is even part of why I am writing this book now. I share these details of my own experience of 9/11 because of the importance of reflexivity in this sort of study. While some of my data is quantitative, some is qualitative and this always calls for analysis of one's biases, experiences, motives and positionality. Most importantly, as the above recounting of my memories of 9/11 make clear, I cannot escape my own identity as an American. I was raised in the military, have served my country overseas (again in the Peace Corps), taught in our nation's juvenile prisons, and identify myself as a patriot. What a complicated word "patriot" has become! This requires me of course to guard against any bias resulting from this positionality. Rather than pretending to an impossible objectivity, I will rather make the strongest case I can for the analysis and conclusions that I will present in the forthcoming chapters.

Each year of teaching in middle or high school following the attacks, on 9/11, I would invite students to share any memories, thoughts or questions they had. My experiences seem typical. I became concerned about the lack of information or incorrect information students have absorbed. Even more concerning was the Islamophobia some exhibited. Reflecting, no doubt, the adults in their lives, some students believed Saddam Hussein was the mastermind behind 9/11. Others reported they had heard former President George W. Bush had had a role. During my time teaching in a northern VA juvenile detention home (2007–2010), my classroom was only a fifteen-minute drive from the Pentagon. Many of my students had personally seen the gaping wound in the Pentagon and the subsequent reconstruction. When I worked at a think-tank in DC, I would pass it each day, amazed anew that security at the bus depot at the Metro's Pentagon station was not

## 4   9/11 and Collective Memory in U.S. Classrooms

tighter. All I needed to be mere feet from the Pentagon itself was metro fare. Like so many others, I visited Ground Zero in the years ensuing; this was in 2006, and so much of the cleaning, clearing and reconstruction had already taken place. Yet the images and emotions of shock, fear, anger and grief remained. One cool spring afternoon of 2002, about seven months after 9/11, I was walking along the National Mall with thousands of others, when the shadow of a small plane glided along the grass. My body tensed and I squinted up at that plane, watching it with anxiety as it flew by the Washington Monument. Only once it had gone by did I realize that those around me were watching the plane as well, apparently thinking along the same horrific lines that I was—a living visualization of collective trauma.

Learning of the 2004 attacks on the pre-school in Beslan, Russia, perhaps also sheds light on the experience of what we might call "indirect" trauma (i.e., trauma that we did not personally experience). Collective trauma is where the personal and the public, even the political, intersect. The reader likely remembers that, after a hostage standoff with Russian authorities, nearly 400 people were killed. About half of the dead were under the age of five. I can recall crying at the news, as perhaps plenty of educators did. During a trip to the grocery store shortly after the Beslan Massacre, I was in view of perhaps it must have been *Time* or *Newsweek*, which of course featured heartrending pictures of besieged children and bereaved parents. The tears flowed as I handed the cashier my Mastercard. Upon reflection, I have to wonder if I would have reacted quite that viscerally in the absence of 9/11. Was there something residual here?

Naturally, the more time passed, the less my students were personally able to recall the attacks of 9/11. At this writing, the year is 2013 and so those born during 2001 are today's 6th or 7th graders. The most immediate connection for them by 2010 or 2011 was having family members deployed in Iraq or Afghanistan, or stories they had been told by parents or other older friends or family. I was not at all surprised that some of my Muslim and/or Arab students spoke of various forms of being stereotyped and discriminated against. By far the most contentious debates we had in class, the ones which most challenged my facilitation skills, were about the role of Islam in American life and in the world. To encourage honest discussion of the role of fear in perpetuating conflict and violence, I would share a story of my own irrational fear with my students. I am embarrassed now to admit how much fear I felt when, on a flight from DC to San Francisco to visit my sister in 2002, only months after the attacks, a middle-aged man in a turban boarded the plane with me. My eyes were on him continuously throughout the flight. Needless to say, all was well, but the shock of realizing how susceptible I was to such irrational fear has stayed with me. Often would I share this story with students hoping my transparency and vulnerability, which I consider to be two traits of effective peace educators, would encourage them to articulate and examine their own fears.

I recount all of this, my own personal experience of that day and its reverberations, since an important theoretical framework for this study on the teaching of 9/11 is historical (or collective) memory (Halbwachs 1992; Volkan 1998, Olick et al. 2011). Coined by Halbswachs, this term refers to how various identity groups, such as a nation, religious group or socio-economic class, collaboratively and collectively interpret their shared past. Based on the examples Halbswach elaborates, collective memory can address a particular event, but it can also address a shared understanding of a particular trend or general reading of history. For example, he suggests that different socio-economic classes have a particular reading of history that is probably not shared in other class groups (120–166). So we need to be careful here—a collective memory is of course not an uncontested memory. To the extent that a particular historical event, like 9/11, generates something we can call consensus, it is important to deconstruct and pull the veil back on how that consensus was developed (or as Foucault would have it, manufactured). One of the most essential outcomes of education is to be able to ask critical questions, tolerate some ambiguity and assess the credibility of information. We must teach students to understand the power dynamics of how history is written and to assess the implications of differing versions of history. In today's classrooms, arguably few events have shaped the lives of our students (and ourselves) more than 9/11 and yet as my research shows, this seminal "before and after" rending of the American story is not being substantively addressed in our classrooms. While some teachers are indeed implementing creative and comprehensive units on 9/11 in their classrooms, this at least based on my own findings remains the exception when it must become the rule. A lack of an historically literate and nuanced understanding of 9/11, I fear, will result in the status quo of ignorance, violence and mistrust between the U.S. and "the Islamic World" being perpetuated. As a colleague commented recently during a conference at which I was presenting this research, 9/11 seems to have become a symbol of the relationship between America and the world's Muslims (American Muslims included). This narrative must urgently be improved if we are to achieve sustainable peace and security.

A post-modern understanding of scholarship does not require us to separate the personal from the empirical, or to hide behind a modernist or positivist notion of detached objectivity. I more often than not find such detached objectivity to be an illusion. This is perhaps especially true when exploring a concept such as collective memory, which is precisely an exploration of how individuals become connected to and find identity and meaning in larger socio-historical events and processes. I am further aware that I myself am a member of the group (Americans) whose collective memory I am studying. This made reflexivity seem especially important. Hence my choice to share at length some of my own personal memories and reflections on 9/11, in and out of the classroom.

## 6    9/11 and Collective Memory in U.S. Classrooms

The question also arises do I actually remember what I believe I remember? Much has been written on the instability, unreliability and ephemeral nature of memory (Engel 1999, Roberts 2002, Sturken 1997). I have personal and professional journals I can look back at for verification of memory and details. Media coverage was of course constant and memorial coverage occurs each year on 9/11. Yet our knowledge of how memory actually works, both personally and collectively, compels me to wonder how accurate my memory is. Some of the details would not amount to much, such as if the strawberry blonde in 7th period who brought me the 9/11 vigil pictures from around the world, was actually perhaps in 6th period. Memories of mine such as standing in line to donate blood and being turned away because the donation sites were overwhelmed by the response could be confirmed by other people. Similar reports were in the media as well. On the weekend after 9/11 (9/11 was a Tuesday) one evening I visited a friend at her house. A flag flew in front of every suburban townhouse on her street. At dusk that night, neighbors emerged carrying flags, candles and lighters in what was part of a national vigil. I had not recalled that the vigil was national, in fact, until research for this book refreshed my memory. This exemplifies how collective memory is shaped and navigated collaboratively in ways of which we are often consciously unaware. Collective memory is, in a complicated way, both individual and social, with both shared and personal aspects. For me, again, a major impulse shaping what 9/11 meant for me was as an educator. For my friend, it was as a parent and, significantly, as an Iranian-American. In fact, she shared with me a story of her brother being harassed by officials at airports, one tale of thousands more like it, which shape the collective memory of 9/11.

Others aspects of my own 9/11 narrative, such as my perceived clear memory of my father's certainty that WWIII had started, seem more suspect. I remember it clearly, but would he? Would he also recall expressing the wish to reenlist in the Army? Did he in fact say this or is the memory my subconscious expression of a daughter's fear? The nature of memory itself does not permit me be to certain without confirmation. We live our lives as narratives. We do not just tell stories. We are stories. For this reason it is crucial that we empower students to internalize this truth, articulate their own stories, empathize with those of others, and interpret why certain people might tell a particular history in such a different way. We often think of these sorts of qualities as values, and in some sense this is true, but in an important pedagogical sense, these qualities in a person are also skills. They can be taught.

### SHAPERS OF COLLECTIVE MEMORY

Collective memory, as we have said, refers to the way in which a social group (typically an ethnic, cultural or political group) recalls and makes meaning around a particularly significant event in their history. Typically, this would be a deeply traumatic event, such as military occupation, genocide or civil war—or of course, a terrorist attack. Through various social, political and economic mechanisms, process or institutions, the narratives of the collective trauma are diffused throughout the society. These institutions are often stakeholders in, or even direct parties to, whatever conflict led to the traumatic event. They include of course governments, who typically seek to codify their own narrative of the conflict into the "set" historical record (Passerini 2005, Cole 2007). Everything from history textbooks to news coverage of the event in question, to museums or memorials that shape the narrative of what happened for future generations, can be implicated in this process of transgenerational trauma, which will be discussed at more length below (Volkan 1998). I am struck by the fact that many of the key institutions relevant to shaping and diffusing collective memory—family, faith institutions, schools, the media—are present in my own vignette. These institutions, as others have also observed, link the micro to the macro, the personal to the political. They are the sites where collective memory is shaped, contested and negotiated.

Surprisingly, while volumes have been written about 9/11, very little of it has yet explored the events of that day through the lens of chosen trauma and subsequent transgenerational transmission of trauma. Some of it has discussed the political and military response from various political perspectives (Bacevich 2013). Other works examine intelligence failures and similar topics leading up to 9/11 (Clarke 2009). Some works tell the story of particular families or survivors. There are some works which deal with the longer term, profound cultural impact of 9/11 and how it has arguably transformed America (Faludi 2007, Morgan, et al. 2009, Alden 2008). Some works discuss 9/11 as related to the cultural myths legitimizing American militarism both before and after 2001 (Muller-Fahrenholz 2006, Hughes 2004). Investigative journalists Dana Priest and William Arkin document the stunning proliferation of the national security state in direct response to 9/11—the vast sums of money and seeming inability to question government leadership that they describe is indicative of collective trauma (Priest and Arkin 2011). Yet none of these take the approach of viewing 9/11 through the lens of chosen trauma. Next I will examine this theory, and then why I believe 9/11 can usefully be seen as a chosen trauma. I will then relate this to the importance of understanding the collective narrative students are receiving about 9/11 in the classroom.


## CHOSEN TRAUMA THEORY

To date, an impressive amount of work has been accomplished on this intersection of collective memory and conflict resolution, especially by peace educators and dialogue facilitators interested in understanding

# 8    9/11 and Collective Memory in U.S. Classrooms

how one generation bequeaths, if you will, the memory of a particular shared trauma to the following generation. Volkan, Julius and Montville (1990) applied theories and concepts of psychodynamics to the understanding of international relations. Volkan (1998) seminally referred to this process of one generation inheriting the chosen trauma of their parents as "trans-generational transmission" (p. 43). Transgenerational trauma is a key building block of his theory of chosen trauma and describes how parents, teachers, media figures, community leaders and political officials can instill in the next generation the trauma of their experience, as well as the enemy images, emotions of hostility and fear, biases, and often Manichean worldview, especially with regards to a perceived enemy. In some instances, this is a largely unconscious process. Volkan, the father of this theory who writes from a psychoanalytic perspective, describes the process of transgenerational trauma like so: "Core personal and large-group identity processes become intertwined when the reservoirs that receive the children's unintegrated "good" self- and object-images and associated affects have two characteristics: (1) they are shared by all children in the large group; and (2) they are constant" (Volkan 2005). As young people grow and are socialized into the values, history, culture and mythology of their large group, they understand that both their physical and psychic security depends on the security of their large group—what Volkan calls their "ethnic tent" (1998). Children competently learn these cultural rules for who they are, who they are not and what is expected to matter to them: "A child's investment in his or her large group depends on what factors the adults in the large group collectively perceive as most important: ethnicity (I am an Arab), religion (I am a Catholic), nationality (I am a German), or a combination of these" (Volkan 2005). It need not be explicitly taught, but often is, both in and out of school. Further we know from research on trauma healing that parents and children can inadvertently re-traumatize one another by one family member witnessing the trauma of the other (O'Donnell and Powers, qtd. in Morgan 2009). Even more importantly for my argument that September 11 is becoming a chosen trauma, this research shows that mere family exposure to the trauma is associated with higher feelings of generalized "social mistrust" (164). If we take the nation, our powerfully imagined community, as a kind of symbolic family, one can easily see how a rupture in the psychic security blanket such as 9/11 would result in such social mistrust. Particularly with constant media reports of sleeper cells, near misses such as the would-be Time Square Bomber, the would-be Christmas Bomber, the would-be Shoe Bomber, and so forth, the socio-psychic wounds have had scant chance to heal.

The role of the media (Silberstein, 2002) has been usefully addressed (though much more remains to be understood). Much like parents and

## Classrooms, and a Country, Cope 9

children dealing with trauma, research suggests that repeated exposure to traumatic events like 9/11 can measurably re-traumatize. News media played the actual footage of the planes crashing into the Twin Towers on a near endless loop. Embedded reporters brought us the bombing of Kabul and the "shock and awe" devastation of Baghdad in real time. Locicero et al. (qtd. in Morgan 2009) write that "repeatedly experiencing the traumatic event" either directly or indirectly is associated with symptoms of PTSD. While they report that only those directly impacted by 9/11 were "triggered" for PTSD by repeated media reports, they also point out the following: " Some of the persistence of the deleterious psychological effects of the terrorist attacks is a function of societal changes related to the attacks rather than the purely lingering effects of the attacks proper. The wars in Iraq and Afghanistan, terror alerts, and changes in airport security contribute to the ongoing effects" (qtd in Morgan 2009 pp. 97–113). This finding, in my view, cannot be over-emphasized. It speaks to how we have allowed 9/11 to seep through the fabric of our collective everyday lives. 9/11 is now a prominent feature of our national story. Further, Locicero et al. note that at the time of their study, 4% of the U.S. was diagnosable with PTSD related to 9/11 (p. 104). We are reminded of the fear and pain of that day every time we listen to a political speech, watch the news or go through airport security. Whether one finds these security measures to be worthwhile and effective or not, the point remains that they contribute to a culture of fear. For these reasons, I argue that 9/11 is best viewed as a chosen trauma and peace builders can respond as such. 9/11 is an era, not just a day.

In other examples of chosen trauma and transgenerational transmission, a nation's (or other culture-sharing group) youth are explicitly charged with undertaking revenge, or at least a refusal to surrender, perhaps by military leaders, media or other cultural figures, faith leaders or family members. In the most extreme examples, the trauma of the conflict, and the resulting emotions of grief, rage and fear, can come to dominate a society's worldview. This results in a group viewing their enmity towards the "other" as central to their worldview and identity. In such a case, the notion and process of "releasing" one's trauma (to the extent possible) and forgiving some of history's worst atrocities might well be experienced as an existential threat. Such dynamics are apparent in the Rwandan genocide, the Bosnian genocide in 1990s, the conflict between Israel and the Palestinians, cases around which much of the literature on peacebuilding and collective memory centers.

Time collapse is a second key theoretical component of understanding chosen trauma (Volkan 1998, p. 35). This phenomenon occurs when a person or group has not been able to properly process and mourn a loss. Hence the original trauma is experienced and re-experienced in a "time collapse" as though it had just occurred. This explains why, for example, UN peacekeepers arrived in Sarajevo to hear a *casus belli* articulated

10  *9/11 and Collective Memory in U.S. Classrooms*

referencing the defeat of the Serbs by the Ottomans in the Battle of Kosovo of 1389! Volkan (1998) cites the example of the infamous assassination of Archduke Ferdinand, which of course lit the fuse of WWI. "What is known", writes Volkan about Gavrilo Princip (the assassin), "is that as a teenager he, like most other Serb youths, was filled with the transformed images of Lazar and Milos as avengers . . . By shooting the Archduke felt he was attacking Austria-Hungary, which had replaced the Ottoman Empire as the 'oppressor' and which had tried to suppress the Kosovo spirit. The archduke's visit on the anniversary of the Battle of Kosovo combined two 'oppressors' in a time collapse" (66). From this example we can see that transgenerational trauma and collective narratives of injustice and victimization can be perpetuated for centuries—or lie dormant until some external source of insecurity or an 'identity entrepreneur' such as Slobodan Milosevic draws on narratives of past loss and victimization as an explanation for current deprivation or suffering. Needless to say, these narratives can be exploited by such figures to tragic and outrageous effect—but these identity entrepreneurs cannot create these narratives 'ex nilio', as I have observed elsewhere (Duckworth 2011). The Milosevics of the world need to draw on narratives, events, myths and symbols that will speak to an experienced collective trauma and offer past enemies as a present scapegoat. In this sense they generate a "narrative motivation" for continuing the conflict. Past chosen traumas around which a group centers its identity provides the fodder.

This concept of the "failure to mourn" can be usefully critiqued in that it does not speak to the sorts of systemic social and political transformations necessary to address the roots of the conflict (and thereby in fact foster healing). Nor does it always specify links between past trauma and present manifestations of systemic (structural) violence. This risks psychologizing the analysis, implying that with sufficient time and therapy, peace can be achieved, failing to address policies, institutions and other tangible systems that must be changed for resolution to occur. Yet the theory does usefully speak to narratives, myths and symbols beyond the material injustices that may provide motivation for being mobilized in a conflict—what I called above "narrative motivation", linking the individual to the public. This systemic application of chosen trauma, we should note, does take us beyond what Volkan himself has done; my hope here is to suggest more macro-level transformations that might foster healing after 9/11. Transformation of curriculum and pedagogy is our focus here; still we should note that a number of other transformations to do with global economics, international institutions and political regimes are needed as well. Schools are only one part of the peace and conflict system; that said for the sake of clarity, other social and political transformations are outside the scope of this work.

Volkan views the process of chosen trauma as below (2002).

Chosen Trauma: Processes and Functions:

Chosen Trauma

↓

Transgenerational Transmission

↓

Change of Function

↓

Ethnic Marker
(a psychological gene of the large group)

↓

Reactivation of Chosen Trauma

↓

Enhancement of Leader-Follower Interaction

↓

Time Collapse

↓

Entitlement for Revenge or Revictimization

↓

Magnification of Current Large-Group Conflict

↓

"Irrational" Decision-Making

↓

Mobilization of Large-Group Activities

## 12  9/11 and Collective Memory in U.S. Classrooms

Given the mass violence that has been promulgated at least in part by the reality of chosen traumas (and present injustices), I would argue that the field must continue elaborating the role of collective trauma in protracted conflicts. There has not yet been much theoretical exploration of 9/11 as a chosen trauma as I noted above (the event is fairly recent by historical standards), so I offer this study as a contribution to this literature. I believe that we must urgently understand what collective narrative about 9/11 is being shaped and what the implications of this narrative are (if one can be indeed identified) for the future of the conflict between the U.S. and 'the Islamic World'. Violent conflicts often possess a self-sustaining dynamic and collective memories of trauma, once entrenched, are incredibly difficult to change. Identities shape conflict and conflicts shape identities. This becomes even truer when a particular narrative or memory is highly salient to the group's identity as 9/11 has been to the U.S. . Hence the importance of understanding the victim narrative the first post-9/11 generation is inheriting. This book, of course, contributes to this effort by empirically examining how 9/11 is being taught in U.S. middle and high school classes.

### 9/11 AS A CHOSEN TRAUMA

I believe that the attacks of 9/11 have become, in the ensuing decade since 2001, a 'chosen trauma' for most Americans (and perhaps by extension our allies) (Volkan 1998, pp. 48–49). Volkan has briefly made the same argument himself (Volkan 2002). That is, the events of that terrible day have become an historical fulcrum around which one can divide U.S. (and world?) history into before and after. Consider, for example, that in writing this text, all I need to do is refer to "9/11", without any further specificity, and my meaning is understood. It was an event that created an era. This suggests the centrality of the attacks of September 11 to American identity since that day. Understanding 9/11 as a chosen trauma, and therefore the dangerous potential for transgenerational transmission of trauma, is a major motivation of mine in writing this book. What this means then is that unless classrooms (and other institutional shapers of national identity like the media or faith communities) can address this collective trauma, the conflict between the U.S. and the "Islamic World" will almost certainly be perpetuated.

To understand the reality of 9/11 as a chosen trauma, then, we must understand the 9/11 era. How has our culture—our schools, our media, creative culture, our political institutions—responded to the first attack on our soil since Pearl Harbor? These realities of America after 9/11 all suggest a nation transformed by trauma. Chosen trauma theory would predict therefore that the current violent and protracted conflict between the U.S. and the Islamic World (recalling my prior cautions about that tricky label) is likely to continue unless the trauma on all sides can be addressed and healed. While this alone will not be sufficient for a sustainable peace, it is essential. Therefore it is urgent for the field of peace building to more deeply understand:

1. To what extent this trauma of 9/11 does in fact have meaningful impact in the daily political life of America's imagined community?
2. How said trauma has impacted U.S. official behavior with respect to the wider conflict between the U.S. and the "Islamic World"?
3. What narrative (if any) is being collectively shaped about what happened on 9/11 and what that means for America's understanding of itself and its role in the world?
4. What sorts of social, political and institutional transformations are necessary to address the root causes of the conflict between the U.S. and the "Islamic World"?
5. Given that we know collective memories (especially traumatic ones related to conflict) can be transmitted to the next generation via media, political institutions, families, faith institutions and schools, what narrative, if any, do we see shaped specifically in classrooms?

While each of the above questions is urgent for peace-building in the 21st century, and each will be addressed in the following chapters, this work focuses primarily on the fifth question which addresses how 9/11 is being taught.

That 9/11 has become a chosen trauma is a contested idea, so I will elaborate here. The defining feature of a chosen trauma is that it becomes the new core of a group's collective identity. Again, this is because the trauma and loss are not successfully processed and healed, with a sense of human security reasonably restored. Much of the literature on collective trauma has also come out of Holocaust studies. Other literature on the role of historical memory and conflict resolution also examines divided Cyprus (Zembylas 2008). There is literature which examines how, for example, African Americans collectively remember centuries of slavery (Kachun 2003, Blight 2002). Can one terrorist attack, then, as horrific and unprecedented for the U.S. as it was, constitute an example of a "chosen trauma"? I would argue yes. Consider, for example, how U.S. foreign policy was reshaped in response to 9/11. *Washington Post* journalists Priest and Arkin, in a series of articles, documented the dramatic growth of the U.S. security and surveillance state, something many Americans would never have accepted were it not for 9/11 (Priest and Arkin 2011). There is not hard evidence I can offer for this, but I find it difficult to imagine Americans willing to take their shoes off to board a plane on September 10, 2001. One particularly striking fact on the growth of the security state since 9/11 is that "Some 1,271 government organizations and 1,931 private companies work on programs related to counterterrorism, homeland security and intelligence in about 10,000 locations across the United States" (Priest and Arkin

14 *9/11 and Collective Memory in U.S. Classrooms*

2011). This report also notes that the U.S. budget for intelligence more than doubled immediately after September 11. After 9/11, a poll by the NYT/CBS found that "80% of the American public was in favor of indefinite detention for noncitizens who threatened national security, 70% favored government monitoring of conversations between suspected terrorists and their lawyers; 64% favored giving the President the authority to change rights guaranteed by the Constitution" (Pyszcznski et al. 2003, p. 99). Pyszcznski et al. make the same observation here that I do: surely Americans would not have felt so before 9/11. It is on these profound structural changes to our democracy that I most squarely rest my argument that 9/11 is (or at least is becoming) a chosen trauma. One need not measure PTSD rates above a certain percentage of the population, or be able to identify linking objects (as in psychoanalysis).

Beyond political and security institutions, however, some have argued that the chosen trauma of 9/11 impacted the wider culture, causing a sort of collective regression that typifies societies dealing with chosen trauma. Susan Faludi, for example, in her impressive *The Terror Dream: Myth and Misogyny in an Insecure America,* argues persuasively that social and political advances made by the feminist movement were consistently challenged or even attacked as a source of U.S. weakness and vulnerability. Feminists, she notes, were attacked and demonized as a security threat, given prevalence of the misogynist view that national security depends on the dominance of masculinist, even militant, values.

Volkan also notes that this mistrust and repression of women is a symptom of societal regression, an indicator of large-group trauma (Volkan, 2002). Hence, this logic goes, women's advances into traditionally male domains emasculates men and renders them less able to secure the nation. This is especially true of women's (intermittent) advances into the realm of national and global security. The irrationality of this search for enemies within itself suggests trauma and extends to other marginalized groups besides women. A traumatized, regressed society typically needs be staunchly vigilant about the policing of its boarders, as Alden documents in his *The Closing of the American Border* (2008) which details how difficult it has now become to immigrate to—or sometimes even visit!—the U.S. While there has always been mistrust of immigrants, and forms of discrimination against them, the overall historic trend of the U.S. has been openness to new immigrants. Also, as hardly need be said, twelve years after the attacks, the U.S. remains embroiled in war in Afghanistan (and some would argue still Iraq as well, though this is debatable). Unofficial U.S. wars brew in Yemen, Somalia, Pakistan and Iran (Scahill 2013). As is at last being reported in the mainstream press, President Obama has significantly increased the number of drone strikes particularly in Pakistan, Yemen and Somalia, though there has barely been any official acknowledgement of this. An unprecedented crackdown on whistleblowers is underway. And, as of yet, any sequester-related cuts to the defense budget have not materialized. Taken together, all of these suggest a society that still feels terrorized.

The above sketches a significant national response to 9/11 at a variety of government and cultural levels. But we should be careful here not to confuse the U.S. government response with the views and feelings of all Americans; this is never the case, even in a democracy. How then do most Americans view the ongoing threat of terror? As Mueller and Stewart note, an average American's statistical likelihood of being killed in a terrorist attack on U.S. soil is one in 3.5 million (Mueller and Stewart 2012, p. 96). This is, as the authors note, at odds with the perception of Americans regarding their risk of being the victim of a terror attack. The authors report that 35%–40% of Americans experience continued fear of a terror attack. A stunning 70% of the Americans in the Gallup survey they cite responded that they consider another terror attack "very or somewhat likely" (Muller and Stewart 2012, p. 108). Other researchers have documented the traumatic fallout from 9/11. In their research, Cohen, Kasen and Chen argue that general increases in public anxiety related to 9/11 are indeed measurable (Cohen et al. 2006, 251–260). Comfortingly, their data shows that trauma symptoms often abate over time, but to conclude from this that there is no chosen trauma is misleading. The abatement of symptoms in individuals is not the only criteria. What matters most for my argument of 9/11 as a chosen trauma is political culture, policies and institutions, especially security institutions. These may or may not change as times goes by, and nearly all we know about the nature of bureaucracies (Arendt 1973, Weber 1947, Cloke 2008) suggests that they do not change on their own.

Cohen and team further write of 9/11.

Unlike previous disasters, this threat has an expected extended duration with no end in sight, including local as well as geographically distant peril. These events were followed closely by the war in Afghanistan in October, anthrax contamination through the postal service and the run up to the war in Iraq, which started in March 2003. Thus policy discussion and actions have kept this issue current and mental health effects potentially ongoing. These data suggest that effects on psychiatric symptoms were visible again as media and political coverage of the 9/11 attacks peaked around the anniversaries of these events. (Cohen et al. 2006)

Their data show an increase in mental-health issues and PTSD (or similar symptoms) related to 9/11. While they argue for caution in interpreting the data from one study, which is always wise, they do also note that geographical proximity to the attacks (New York, DC or PA) was not found to be necessary to exhibit trauma symptoms. The trauma therefore was found to be more generalized; one did not need to have experienced it directly to be impacted.

## 16  *9/11 and Collective Memory in U.S. Classrooms*

In other words, it is important to understand 9/11 not as one attack on one day, but rather as an entire set of events as well that have occurred in response to 9/11. This includes, of course, the subsequent wars which both proved at least in my reading unwinnable, the anthrax attacks, the torture memos, the PATRIOT Act and numerous other events. Relatedly, we need to understand 9/11 as one event in a wider conflict between the U.S. and extremists employing the ideology of Islam, which began far before 2001.

Again, I assert that 9/11 is becoming a chosen trauma for the United States. Chosen trauma theory states that when a society experiences a mass historical trauma, that group's collective identity can be reshaped and centered around the trauma such that the event in question becomes a lens through which all else is seen. This is manifest in the explicitly articulated sense of so many Americans (myself included) that everything changed after September 11. Logically, as a result of chosen trauma, resources are redirected primarily towards security. This is the case post-9/11 in America, as I documented above. Another manifestation of chosen trauma is that other social groups are sorted into ally or enemy based on the event in question, a dynamic clearly visible in U.S. foreign policy post-9/11. Commonly "enemy images" emerge and are disseminated throughout the culture (via the above-noted mechanisms of schools, media and other similar mechanisms). Enemy images, as the term suggests, are images each conflict group forms of the "Other" as a result of the pain and trauma of the conflict. Dehumanization of the enemy group is almost always the result, as the common examples of the Holocaust or the Rwandan genocide teach. Regarding September 11, I am reminded here of the recent spike of attacks on Muslim mosques, according to the Council on American-Islamic Relations (CAIR online). The strange controversy surrounding the Mosque in Manhattan, too near to some minds to Ground Zero, is a further example. A number of elected officials in the U.S. have advocated for anti-Sharia laws, as for example reported by the Detroit Free Press (Goodman 2012). Representative Peter King (R-NY) held Congressional hearings on possible Islamic radicalization of Americans (Farenthold and Boorstein, 2011).

Chosen traumas often result in a cycle of violence and enmity between the group perceiving themselves to be the victim and the group they perceive to be the perpetrator of their trauma. This cycle has been manifest between the U.S. and the Islamic World since 9/11 as the overseas escalations, domestic Islamophobia and continued attempts to attack American civilians demonstrate. Through political and socio-cultural mechanisms such as schooling, the media, museums, memorials and explicit government policies, this trauma is at risk of being inherited by successive generations. Correspondingly, the conflict will continue to escalate and expand, taking on the self-sustaining dynamic typical of protracted social conflicts.

If 9/11 has indeed become a chosen trauma for Americans, as I argue it has, the realities of transgenerational trauma suggest that it is urgent that we understand how the first post-9/11 generation (today's middle and high schoolers) understands the events of that day. As a survey by the Center for American Progress reported, Americans born between 1978 and 2000, and the generation after them (post-millennials)—considers the terrorist crimes committed on September 11 to be the most significant public event of their lifetime. The generation after them will not recall or experience a pre-9/11 world. As the reflection of one millennial journalist noted, "Millennials have lived most of our adult lives in a world of increased security measures" (Towns 2011). What sort of relationship with their government will this generation forge? What sort of relationship with "with Islamic World" will they expect from their leaders?

We must know whether the narrative about 9/11 being shaped for them is likely to foster continued war or facilitate peace (or both in some complex manner). When such narratives remain unexamined, or invisible, they can contribute to the perpetuation of the conflict without the parties being adequately empowered to assess how the conflict began and what choices are truly in one's best interest as regards continuing with the conflict or not. There have certainly been attempts to grapple with the collective meaning of 9/11—Hollywood movies such as *Flight 93* or *World Trade Center*, news documentaries, museum exhibits, various dialogues hosted by houses of worship or universities. While these are all important parts of understanding how 9/11 is in the process of being internalized in the collective memory of Americans, schools are too often overlooked in these analyses, yet they are significant shapers of our personal and political identity (Zembylas 2008, McGlynn et al. 2009; Duckworth, Williams and Allen 2012). Schools are one of the most important points of nexus between the micro and the macro, and powerfully influence how we as citizens view our national identity and role in the world. To interrupt chosen trauma, schools must be a part of the peacebuilding narrative intervention.

One observation throughout the literature on trauma and conflict is that victims often need to feel that their experience of suffering has been unique. This seems to be true of both groups and individuals. The danger here is that this entails a denial, at least an implied denial, of the possible victimhood of other groups. Perhaps as a result of the trauma, victims appear to feel threatened by the thought of acknowledging the trauma of others, especially when that "other" is the group they perceive to have caused their grief and loss. This treats trauma as a "zero sum" game. John Mack (1971) referred to this as the "egoism of victimization". This is surely due to the humiliation and sense of invisibility and powerlessness involved in trauma. Victims, their leaders and their progeny promise themselves that they will not be victims again. Dominating as much socio-political space as possible, insisting on being heard and valued, can result. When a group has experienced a humiliation, what the literature refers to as "reversing" the humiliation becomes a necessary part of healing. Such a dynamic makes dialogue and resolution quite difficult, especially when resolution must entail acknowledgement of the other group's own suffering. Needless to

# 18    9/11 and Collective Memory in U.S. Classrooms

say, this becomes even truer when one's own group has been the cause of said trauma suffered by another group.

This is because to do so would be to fundamentally challenge a particular group's narrative about two key aspects of identity as it relates to a particular conflict. One aspect is who a particular group believes they are as a people. Historical processes, current political, cultural and economic dynamics, stories and myths that have shaped the civic religion, group values, and so forth are all aspects of this group identity. The second aspect is how group members understand what took place during the particular conflict and why they behaved as they did—what I call a conflict group's *narrative motivation*. Conflict narratives serve a purpose of justification. As Cobb writes, "The struggle is a struggle not just for survival but for legitimacy, moral legitimacy" (Cobb 2003, p. 104). The conflict resolution literature refers to these as "justice narratives" (Cobb 2003, p. 105). The U.S. has told such a "justice narrative" to itself, and to the world community, with respect to the invasion of Afghanistan, the invasion of Iraq, detentions in Guantanamo Bay, drone strikes in numerous countries and arguably even the harsh punishment of whistleblowers whose leaks have related to national security (such as Chelsea Manning, former State Department officer Peter Van Buren or Gen. John Allen).

In such a case of protracted, violent macro-conflict, a narrative transformation process to begin resolving the conflict may imply more than transforming the narrative each conflict party tells about a certain conflict. The larger group identity itself may ultimately need to be transformed for sustainable resolution, or at least the narrative they tell themselves and others about the conflict. As Cobb writes, we need to understand more about what types of intervention would "support the evolution" of large-group identities, especially "in the context of a given, very complex conflict where power must be addressed as a part of the diagnosis of the conflict" (Cobb 2003, p. 99). Group identities and the narratives which emerge from and are embedded in them of course are related. Thus to transform the conflict, one must evolve both the narrative the group tells about the conflict and perhaps even the group identity itself (or at least aspects of the group's identity). I would argue, of course, that peace education is one such method of narrative intervention. Peace education (at its best) has the ability to engage and challenge current conflict narratives, facilitate the development of new narratives, and help develop respectful and trusting relationships across conflicting community groups. Hence the focus of this book on the importance of schools and curriculum for conflict transformation. I will elaborate on this throughout Chapter 2.

Narratives are essential to understanding and resolving conflict (Cobb 2003, Lederach 2005, Duckworth 2011). Especially in the context of a violent conflict, with heightened emotion and deep, historical mistrust, to allow for any truth in the other's narrative can seem like disavowing one's own truth. This is of course not something most of us can do easily. The context of a conflict in which enemy images have developed make this even more difficult. Enemy images can emerge in any conflict, but protracted, violent political-ethnic conflicts seem especially prone to them and the conflict between the U.S. and the Islamic World is no exception. In such a heightened stage of conflict escalation, groups can thoroughly dehumanize the Other, stripping them of any human dignity or morality. Groups may even come to see one another as a manifestation of evil itself, as in the case of the Rwandan genocide (Sentana 2009). Further, enemy images can take on a "mirror" quality, in which at least according to psychoanalysis, those qualities we hate most in ourselves, we project onto the Other. Hence, at least according to this genocidal logic, to destroy the Other is to destroy evil (Volkan 1998). This narrative violence must end if we are to minimize the risk of future physical violence. For the narrative violence to end, the narratives which the parties to the conflict tell about themselves and one another, and the histories they have endured together, must be transformed.

Much of the literature on chosen trauma and conflict narratives also speaks to the terrible power of humiliation which is often a central theme in conflict narratives. Humiliation burns and lasts. It seems to be experienced by conflict parties even as an existential threat—which stands to reason if we agree with Burton (1990) that esteem is a basic human need. Along these lines, I have written on dignity as a basic human need (Duckworth 2011), and view dignity and humiliation as opposites. To restore psychological, social and perhaps even physical security, we must insist on dignity. To the minds of some victims of humiliation, this entails inflicting humiliation in return on the aggressor. This is the essence of the cycle of revenge that can characterize so many conflicts.

On September 11, 2001, clearly the U.S. experienced the first violation of its borders since Pearl Harbor as a humiliation. Just as clearly, groups espousing various forms of political or militant Islam see U.S. power, as well as a long history of colonial occupation, in the Middle East (and elsewhere) as a humiliation. All conflicts have the following in common: both parties argue that their own actions have been defense, not offense. This is certainly true of both the U.S. and of Islamic terror groups, both of whom have argued that they are on the defensive, responding to the other's provocations. This is the narrative justification for a group's or individual's actions during a conflict, often a justification for atrocities—what I called above a conflict group's *narrative motivation*.

Chosen trauma is more than "learning to hate" at the knee of one's parent. Chosen trauma theorists describe it as a collective, largely unconscious process that can persist over the course of centuries. As Volkan writes,

> There is far more to transgenerational transmission of chosen trauma than children mimicking the behavior of parents or hearing the stories of the event told to them by the older generation, nor is it merely a matter of transgenerational sympathy, powerful as that emotion may

## 20   *9/11 and Collective Memory in U.S. Classrooms*

be. Rather, it is the end result of mostly unconscious psychological processes by which children's core identities are flooded with and therefore influenced by the injured self- and internalized object-images and associated affects that rightfully belong to the original victims, caregivers or parents. (2002, pp. 456–483).)

Eventually being a part of the experience of the chosen trauma itself is what links members to the larger group, key to identifying someone as either an identity group member—or not. Accordingly a central part of contemporary Jewish identity is what one knows and how one relates to Israel and the Holocaust. Memories of, involvement in and/or knowledge of Civil Rights and Jim Crow form a key aspect of African American identity. If I am correct about 9/11 becoming (or having already become) a chosen trauma for Americans, what we should see then is relating to, and grieving, the traumatic terrorist attacks of 9/11—of having suffered on that day in some manner whether you were there or not—as a manifestation of the strength of one's identity as an American. The danger here is that this can cast a desire for revenge as a barometer of one's patriotism. In my view, this is readily observable in both our culture and our politics since September 11, 2001. As Volkan writes, such chosen traumas can shape international relations: "Awareness of the chosen traumas of groups in conflict can enlarge our understanding about how they may become the fuel to ignite the most horrible human dramas and/or keep the fire going once hostilities start" (Volkan 2002). If we fail to understand the chosen trauma of 9/11, I fear it will prove fodder for future conflict. History shows that political leaders are all too skilled at sensing and using chosen traumas to rally people for conflict.

Chosen trauma, according to Volkan, involves two basic steps: one is a "failure to mourn" and the second is a collective, or large scale, regression. Volkan of course is applying basic psychoanalytic theories to large-scale socio-political groups. Despite my criticisms above that this aspect of Volkan's theory can overlook the need for systemic and institutional transformation, it is an important aspect of how chosen trauma works. The failure to mourn results in an inability to heal and process one's grief. Collective regression can then follow. Hence two questions that might usefully guide us in determining if the 9/11 has indeed become a chosen trauma for the U.S. would be if America has successfully mourned our collective loss and if we have exhibited signs of large-scale regression.

Have we indeed then failed to mourn 9/11? Bear in mind, a society can recover from a particular trauma while those most directly impacted have not fully mourned their loss (of a child, a husband or wife). We all wish Godspeed to their healing but surely one is never quite the same after such a loss. My point here is a bit different. Have we mourned and at least begun to heal *as a collective*? Have we begun the necessary social and political transformations to address the root of the conflict? Given the way it

*Classrooms, and a Country, Cope*  21

dominates our politics even still, given how it has reshaped our government and political culture, and considering that so many of us (myself included) see 9/11 as a "before and after" in U.S. history, I must conclude that we have not yet successfully mourned our collective loss on that day. We have not returned to a sense of security or normalcy. O'Donnell and Powers ( qtd in Morgan, 2009) note that ambiguous loss can lead to protracted grief. That is, those directly impacted by 9/11 who did not for a long time (or perhaps still do not) know the fate of their loves ones experience much difficulty mourning, even after decades. I wonder if this is "scalable" to the imagined community of America in the sense of the ambiguity of understanding the impacts of 9/11 or even the full extent of our loss. As recently as April 2013, excavations at Ground Zero begun again, in the hopes of learning more by recovering further remains, according to CBS News ("39 Possible" online). This further suggests that we have not yet fully mourned this collective trauma. Not only can victims' families not yet heal without certainty, in a very real sense nor can the "family" of the nation. And as suggested above, the related media coverage will keep 9/11 before the eyes and in the ears of Americans. Certainly, too, the social and political questions raised by 9/11, especially regarding the proper balance between freedom and security in a democracy, remain unresolved.

If then we have not yet properly mourned our terrible loss on 9/11, chosen trauma theory offers one disquieting suggestion as to why not. Based on this theory, the parties in a conflict characterized by chosen trauma are in an oddly intimate relationship. Often the "other", as classic psychoanalysis would have it, symbolizes to us all of the qualities in ourselves that we most hate and fear. It is argued this is why conflicts whose narratives involve chosen trauma feature such violence. To destroy the "other" is to destroy (de-story) the most hated parts of ourselves. In a complicated way then, extrapolating from Volkan, to fully mourn the losses of 9/11 would entail confronting all of the ambivalence and sometimes outright hostility within mainstream U.S. culture towards Islam. Ultimately to fully understand and grieve the events of 9/11 then would be to confront the generations of injustice between the U.S. and "the Islamic World". This work would include confronting Islamophobia, orientalism, and the necessary rebuilding of social, economic and political institutions of predominantly Muslim countries post-colonialism. (This is necessary to create the space needed for "re-storying" to occur.) Proper mourning of 9/11 would further entail confronting anti-Western extremism and the attendant conspiracy theories about how 9/11 actually occurred. (I have in mind here the view that it was a Zionist plot to give the U.S. reason to attack predominantly Muslim countries, for example.) In short, it would involve putting right the mistrustful and violent relationship between the U.S. and the Muslim World. Conflicts are always about a relationship gone wrong.

Chosen trauma theory also suggests that one can detect chosen trauma by analyzing the leadership of the large group in question, and the response

## 22   9/11 and Collective Memory in U.S. Classrooms

of large-group members to that leadership. Volkan observes that a "rally around the leader" phenomenon can indicate chosen trauma. I would agree, although I would add that merely rallying around the leader of one's group, absent other "symptoms", alone probably does not demonstrate the presence of chosen trauma. Certainly we saw such a "rally around the leader" effect in the months after 9/11. President Bush's approval rating soared, vendors ran out of flags to sell and a superpower reoriented to a war footing, where we have remained since that day. By 2004, Bush's approval rating was much lower, as one would expect. By this time, he along with both houses of Congress had passed the PATRIOT Act, with the full support of both Democrats and Republicans, which enabled indefinite detention, begun creating CIA "black sites" in countries like Egypt and Poland where terror suspects were tortured, wiretapped U.S. citizens without any warrant and of course, taken the nation officially to war via the March 2003 invasion of Iraq. In the context of a campaign that relied heavily on engaging American's security fears, the Bush/Cheney ticket was of course reelected. That does not prove the manifestation of chosen trauma in response to 9/11, but the repeated and explicit use of 9/11 by various candidates of both parties, including Bush and Cheney, is not in dispute. One campaign ad of 2004 gained attention by featuring wolves at prey. "Weakness attracts those who are waiting to do America harm", the narrator intones, warning against the cuts to defense, and especially intelligence, that the ad claims Bush's opponent (John Kerry, now Obama's Secretary of State) supported. Here is where a pack of grey wolves begin sprinting through the forest, clear metaphors for terrorists or other menaces. The ad explicitly states that such cuts are especially dangerous in the world post-9/11. It is worth noting here that this was an official campaign add, approved at the ad's end by President Bush.

An exhaustive survey of such examples from various campaigns after September 11, 2001, would fill a book of its own. Here I will offer only one more to illustrate my case. Rudy Giuliani, nicked named by supporters (and the media) "Rudy the Rock" for his steel as mayor of New York City in the aftermath of the attack, was a candidate for the Republican nomination in 2008 (McCain of course went on to become the nominee). His penchant for referring to 9/11 throughout every speech on the stump was difficult to miss and in fact became late-night fodder for David Letterman, among others. Another candidate for the nomination invoked the decidedly post-9/11 hero of the T.V. series "24", Jack Bauer, in answering a question about the appropriate use of force when questioning a terrorist. Of course the dynamics of campaigns and voting are complex, and again, I do not argue that a particular candidate's employment of 9/11 or fear more generally explain why he won or lost. My aim here is to draw together evidence of the fear free flowing in the atmosphere since 9/11. Now, over a decade on, I believe it is too easy to forget how much has changed since then. We altered our body politic in fundamental ways as a response to that fear, and yet enough time has passed that those changes may soon become normalized, if they have not already. This is even truer for today's middle and high schoolers, who will not have reliable memories of their own of 9/11 or the world before it.

To continue supporting my contention that 9/11 is becoming a chosen trauma, a brief discussion of the nature of American social and political identity is necessary. At least since WWII, Americans have seen themselves as a powerful, nearly invincible force for good in the world. An undisputed super-power, this position in the world consolidated a national identity as capable, inventive, generous, and righteous. As Rich Rubenstein (2010) persuasively wrote in his *Reasons to Kill: Why Americans Go to War*, Americans are historically rather skeptical of both government and war. Curious then, as he observes, that we seem to have fought so many of them. Why is this? While I cannot summarize his entire argument here, the important part for our purposes is this. Our political leaders have often had to work to convince Americans to go to war, and the rhetoric that seems to have been the most effective throughout U.S. history has been the defense of what we know to be right, particularly when helpless and/or innocent victims are seen as being menaced by a bully or when an argument can be fashioned that frames a particular war as a last resort after all other peaceful alternatives have been exhausted (Rubenstein 2010, 20–22).

September 11 was on the most basic human level a mass-murder and a crime against thousands of individuals and families from eighty-six nations. Yet on the level of political symbolism, it was also an attack on the U.S. position in the world, and America's capitalist democratic ideology, as described above. One underappreciated aspect of Al Qaeda's ideology is their anti-capitalist fervor (Berna 2012). Specifically, 9/11 was an attack on the sense of benevolence and impenetrability which seem a core of American identity. When Americans talk about 9/11, we often refer to the sheer shock it made us feel; it was so terrorizing precisely because it threatened our view of ourselves as invulnerable. One could even think of it, in its large-scale psychological impact, as an attempted reversal of the "chosen glory" of the U.S. and Allied victory in WWII. After all, the post-war era is truly what consolidated American economic, political and cultural hegemony, in large part due to this victory.

Needless to say, fear is a result of mass trauma and it seems obvious that 9/11 evoked (whether rationally or no) a deep fear not just of terrorists without but of a further "enemy within"—hence the fear of immigrants, Muslim Americans and so on daily observable in the headlines and in one's own life. This is reflected both in our news headlines and our culture. "Homeland", "Scandal" and "24" might be considered examples; they all involved heroes (as the show defines such) demonstrating a willingness to use violence and torture in defense of the country. In a recent Angelina Jolie movie entitled "Salt", undercover Soviet spies who had been trained in the U.S. from early childhood come of age to undertake their attacks on the

## 24    9/11 and Collective Memory in U.S. Classrooms

American government, harkening back to an old McCarthy era paranoia. Yet the fear implied here seems to reach even deeper than that, to a strain in U.S. political culture that has always existed in some form: xenophobia. Without clear ethnic, racial or religious boundaries to American national identity, the logic of this fear goes, how is one to know a true American? Many commentators have remarked on this xenophobic strain of U.S. culture, both before and after September 11. It helps explain the internment of Japanese Americans during WWII, the white violence associated with desegregation during the 1960s, the irrational intensity of the fear of especially Hispanic immigrants, and of course, the violence directed at Muslim Americans or those mistaken for Muslim Americans (such as the recent shooting of a number of Sheiks at Oak Creek) especially after the attacks of 9/11. The uglier underbelly of this narrative, of course, is overtly racist, believing that American identity is white.

Consider, for example, the protests in response to what became framed as the "9/11 Mosque", an Islamic worship and community center somewhat near Ground Zero. State and national representatives in various legislatures have attempted to pass (sometimes with success!) laws to "protect" American citizens from what supporters of such legislation see as the threat of Sharia law in the U.S. While comfortingly fringe, a pastor named Terry Jones (in Gainesville, FL), infamously has sponsored "Burn a Quran" days, to such intense media coverage that the Secretary of Defense and the Commander in Chief themselves both had to announce in public that they believed his idea to be a terrible one. Congressman Keith Ellison, who was sworn in as a Muslim on a Koran, was met with protest (Frommer, "Ellison Uses Thomas Jefferson's Quran", Washington Post Online). More recently, a senior advisor to Sec. of State Clinton, Huma Abedin, was openly accused by then-candidate for the Republican nomination for the Presidency, Michele Bachmann (R-MN), of plotting against the U.S. with the Muslim Brotherhood. Most of my readers will also be familiar with prevalent fears that President Obama himself is something of an Al-Qaeda Manchurian candidate. The consistency with which these sorts of phenomenon have occurred since 9/11 are evidence to me of remaining trauma in the fabric of our social and political culture. Satirist Stephen Colbert has highlighted this Islamophobia as a fear of "creeping hummus".

Other scholarship on trauma and 9/11 is useful here—though again, to my knowledge, 9/11 has never been examined through the lens of chosen trauma theory at length. Pyszcznski et al., in their *In the Wake of 9/11* (2003), examine 9/11 through Terror Management Theory. Terror management theory suggests that culture, and specifically the worldviews they teach us, has emerged because of the unique human awareness of death. We have a social and psychological need, therefore, to keep the terror of that impending death at bay throughout our lives. Religion and worldviews, of course a key aspect of culture, helps us understand our place in the universe and address the question of what happens when we die, almost always offering assurances of an afterlife (at least if one has behaved). The result, according to the authors, is that when we encounter those of other cultures, we are forced to face the fact that other worldviews exist and that this implies our own "terror management system" is not the only one. Hence we could be wrong, with our comforting assurances weakened.

What does this have to do with my argument that 9/11 is a chosen trauma? If the authors are correct in their theory—and they do present some convincing empirical data—the trauma of 9/11 could well be deeper than the "mere" piercing of one's sense of security in the world. It could well be deeper even than the U.S. understanding itself in a profoundly transformed way. What trauma management theory suggests for my own argument that 9/11 is a chosen trauma is that the trauma of 9/11 forced many Americans to confront an even more profound, metaphysical, existential terror.

To conclude this thread of argument, several features of the emerging collective narrative seem clear. They resonate deeply with American self-identity and the larger narrative of how we view ourselves and who we are in the world. One feature of the collective narrative of 9/11 is the innocence of not just the victims themselves but of the U.S. as a whole. Few would dispute the innocence of the men and women merely going to work one Tuesday morning, or the innocence of the first responders. My observation is larger. The U.S. as a whole, as a political entity, is deemed innocent. To suggest otherwise in the political climate since 9/11 is to invite accusations of hating America, being a terrorist or at least sympathizing with terrorists. In our collective thinking, we have failed too often to distinguish between *analysis* and *justification*. This has done us, in my view, the disservice of being able to rationally analyze what responses to 9/11 are in fact in the national interest. Given our nature as a democracy, there will always be some dispute about what those policies ought to be. That's healthy. The danger we face moving forward, however, as memory becomes history, is that the severely closed social and political space for robust discussion of what policies are truly the wisest as it relates to global peace and security, counterterrorism and U.S. relations with "the Muslim World" will not reopen. No free society can afford such a dynamic.

The unexpected nature of 9/11 is another fascinating feature of the congealing, collective narrative around the attacks of that day. Again, the myths of our national identity had lead us to believe that we were invincible or immune. Given that Al Qaeda had attacked the U.S. before, and that the Bush administration had memos from the intelligence community that urged action and predicted the attack, arguably this should not be. As most Americans know, the administration received a memo entitled "Bin Laden determined to Strike within the United States". This memo specifically refers to domestic targets and the methodology of hijacking airplanes. (The redacted version of this memo is available here: http://www.fas.org/irp/cia/product/pdb080601.pdf). In language strikingly similar to that which Bush himself would later use post-9/11, Ramzi Yousef

## 26  *9/11 and Collective Memory in U.S. Classrooms*

(a planner of the World Trade Center bombings of the 1990s) referred to "bringing the fight to America", in a painfully classic example of the manner in which conflict parties inevitably position themselves as the victim who is on defense, never offense.

Often collective narratives of a shared trauma are shaped more by grief, fear and rage than by reason. Closed narratives, which leave no room from dissent, diversity of perspectives or collective reflection, will almost certainly escalate the current conflict dynamic. At best, it will serve a dangerous status quo. The same is true of closed narratives which others may hold regarding 9/11 as well—such as the view held by some that the attacks were a "false flag" committed by U.S. and Israel. As recently as 2011, Pew Global noted that "there is no Muslim public in which even 30% accepts that Muslims committed the attacks" ("Muslim Western Tensions" online). Strong psychological defense mechanisms are clearly at work within the minds of both parties. For most Americans no doubt the first Gulf War, the seizure of the Embassy in Tehran in 1979, hostage taking, the attacks on the 1972 Munich Olympics, a nightclub in Berlin the 1980s and frequent attacks in Israel are woven together in a monolithic narrative of Muslims as a bloodyminded and violent people who cannot govern themselves and cannot be trusted in a deal. Similarly drone strikes, the CIA coup in Iran of 1953, the U.S. alliance with Israel and military training and funding of authoritarian security forces in Iraq, Egypt, Bahrain and elsewhere has driven a narrative of Americans as callous, arrogant, insatiably greedy and violent. Neither of these narratives will allow for any sort of productive communication to occur, let alone any sort of sustainable peace building. Direct encounter with one another is necessary, to apply Thich Nhat Hahn's observation. So too is the co-creation of a much larger (more comprehensive), more multi-dimensional narrative regarding the entrenched and escalating conflict between the U.S. and "the Islamic World". As we will see when we hear from teachers themselves, the narrative students receive regarding 9/11 is worryingly thin and narrow. This reflects, in my analysis, the increasingly narrow autonomous space teachers have in which to create and implement curriculum with meaningful educational goals and local student needs in mind.


## NEW YORK, DC AND BOSTON: A TALE OF TWO ATTACKS

At times a horrific circumstance will provide an excellent social laboratory for the study of peace and conflict. As I was drafting this book, on mid-day of April 15, 2013, two bombs went off in Copley Square, one of the most major commercial and residential areas of Boston. This area also happens to be known to much of my family as home. All Americans felt the pain and outrage of 9/11, but this one was even more personal for me. My mother, sister, brother-in-law, step dad and four year-old niece were walking near

Copley Square (about two blocks away) home from the Red Sox game they'd just enjoyed. Within an hour, one could see the national habits and myths, both admirable and dangerous, manifest as echoes of 9/11. This was perhaps best put on display by some of the major cable U.S. media (specifically CNN and Fox News) in their failure to accurately report what turned out to be the non-arrest of two suspects reportedly caught on camera. For an afternoon, major cable news networks inaccurately "broke" the news that a suspect/s had been arrested and that an FBI press conference was imminent. It fell to the FBI themselves to correct the story. A couple of days after this, the Bureau did indeed release photos of two suspects, and by the end of the week, one suspect was dead in a shoot out with local law enforcement and the other was in custody.

The particular nature of the media failures here were not just revealing, they were dangerous. One reporter, CNN's John King, felt the need to repeat numerous times in his banter with Wolf Blitzer that the arrest was of a "dark-skinned male". Given that there had not even yet been an arrest, this information could not have been verified via the traditional three separate sources, yet it was repeated. While King and Blitzer did state that they did not have complete certainty, they also clearly reported that a "dark-skinned male" was in fact in custody. King stated, "I was told by law enforcement officials that a dark-skinned male was in custody". The damage resurfaced from the darkest parts of collective American psyche and history, and was a clear reminder of the racist nature of our media even today. In a social and political culture where teenaged Trayvon Martin can be shot simply walking home with a hoodie, such mistakes by the media are not just embarrassing. They are perilous. Less than twelve hours after the bombing, a Saudi man, hospitalized with his wounds from the bombing, had his apartment searched. Shortly after, a Palestinian woman in Boston was assaulted. Another young man, Sunil Tripathi, also misidentified as a suspect by social media, has since committee suicide.

The subtext of the errors was clear: the perpetrators of the Boston bombings were presumed likely black, Hispanic or Middle Eastern. To incorrectly "confirm" this was to confirm what far too many were already primed to believe and to reproduce white privilege and the social oppression of black and brown people. This is important to understanding the collective narratives of 9/11 in the following way. Part of the national myth of American exceptionalism holds that the United States is a uniquely blessed nation, meant by God to represent freedom, human dignity and progress. Thus attacks on U.S. civilians are not merely seen as outrageous crimes, and human rights violations (which they surely are), they are framed almost instantly as attacks on the values of freedom and democracy, even on civilization itself. In moving speeches at the Memorial shortly after the bombing, MA Gov. Duval Patrick and President Obama both invoked this narrative. Obama even specifically referred to America's "state of grace". And Boston itself of course (like Washington DC and New York) is rich with American

## 28  9/11 and Collective Memory in U.S. Classrooms

history and symbolism. Corollary to this national myth is the view of other peoples as at least somewhat less godly, free, modern or brave. This casts ready suspicion on all who might be defined as less or not American. It hardly needs to be said from here that foreigners, immigrants, and those who are not white and Christian have historically been locked into this category. The consequences for Martin and Triparthi were lethal. While it is still too early to judge how we will respond to the Boston Bombing, one can already clearly see the ghosts of 9/11 haunting how we talk about and understand what occurred.

This chapter has discussed the need for and scope of the study. It has specified the questions anchoring the research and begun to sketch out the necessary theoretical framework of chosen trauma. Relatedly it argues that 9/11 has become a chosen trauma for Americans, and that this makes it urgent that we understand the collective narrative of that event that today's young people are receiving.

Chapter 2 will discuss the literature on peace education and historical memory, providing the theoretical framework for this study. It will also review the literature specific to the teaching of 9/11 to ground the study.

Chapter 3 will present the quantitative data gathered from a survey of middle and high school teachers in U.S. schools. This survey will help us to construct a picture of if and how 9/11 is being taught in America's schools.

Chapter 4, similarly, will present the qualitative data, gathered from more in-depth, narrative interviews with teachers regarding how they have addressed 9/11. Here classroom teachers discuss challenges, successes, activities, emotions and barriers they have experienced when teaching such a painful and politicized subject.

Chapter 5 offers analysis specific to the barriers which teachers report facing as they teach 9/11. Such barriers included the emotional and painful nature of the content, political controversies related to the 9/11 era, and most significantly, a bureaucratic culture of centralized curriculum and standardized, scantron testing.

Chapter 6 concludes by reflecting on data drawn from Chapters 3–5. Given what we learned in those chapters about how teachers are addressing 9/11, what can we say overall about how 9/11 is being addressed in the classroom? What narrative are students inheriting? Is this narrative likely to perpetuate further war or facilitate peace? Again, if peace builders are to be able to design any sort of long-term narrative interventions, we must consider the narrative being shaped in classrooms for the generation currently coming up—the first "post-9/11" generation.

# 2 Peace Education, Chosen Traumas and Collective Memory in the Classroom

## PEACE EDUCATION AND HISTORICAL MEMORY

This chapter will review the literature on peace education and collective memory. The intersection of these conceptual building blocks provides key context for understanding how peace educators have approached teaching about especially violent and contested histories. This will then shed light on how teachers can best approach addressing the chosen trauma of 9/11. The literature on chosen trauma, collective memory and peace education is vast, so I will only address the intersection of these literatures here.

Peace education has evolved and adapted over the decades to meet a variety of different needs. Pedagogy and curriculum have addressed critical literacy (Morton in Amster and Ndura, 2009, 45–58), bullying and other forms of school violence (Duckworth 2011, Duckworth, Williams and Allen, 2012), civil wars (Ndura 2009, Ahluwalia, et al. 2012), the root causes of conflict and violence (Bajaj 2008, Morrison and Harris 2003, Davies 2008), development (Bailey in Amster and Ndura 2009) and human rights (Bajaj 2012). Critical peace education has been a central focus; this literature foregrounds the realities of oppression and injustice and views empowerment of those marginalized as central to the goals of peace education (Freire 2003, Duckworth 2012). An increasing amount of the literature on peace education addresses the intersection of peace education and historical memory. Much of this literature is largely conceptual and theoretical. To further build this literature, I have recently been writing on ways in which teachers can implement critical peace education, especially in the amazingly challenging context of a society recovering from civil war, genocide or other forms of mass violence such as 9/11 (Duckworth forthcoming Jan 2015). Two techniques I believe can provide great guidance for teachers on how to address such a devastating event: oral histories and futures visioning.

In fact, as we will see in Chapter 4, some teachers did make use of oral histories. They both invited students to hear oral histories collected by professionals and to gather their own oral histories from older friends and relatives. What's so important about this is that students here are not just

30  *9/11 and Collective Memory in U.S. Classrooms*

"learning" history, they are engaging with it, making meaning as *authors* in a very real sense of history, not just readers of history, as the late Howard Zinn might observe. Dialogue, especially in post-conflict contexts and in intercultural contexts, has been essential to most concepts of peace education. Oral histories allow classroom space for students to explore contested histories and allow students (and teachers) to engage their communities. This empowers them to begin to deconstruct the hegemonic narratives which are likely to be at least in part driving the conflict.

"Futures visioning", as discussed by Elise Boulding (2000), a mother of peace studies, can also be useful, specific means of addressing collective trauma in the classroom. This methodology is an invitation for various diverse societies to envisage together what a future of coexistence might look like. Questions for dialogue might include what shared basic human needs or goals might exist and how to best go about meeting these needs or achieving these goals. Sherif of course referred to such shared goals as superordinate goals (1958). If there is sufficient trust, the inescapable reality of differences can be a part of the dialogue as well. If not, trust-building will have to be the focus of the peace building process.

Yet my application of Boulding's concept here to peace education curriculum implies the need to address the "heavy hand of history" as well as the future. We have a paradox here in that we cannot really move on into our futures without addressing the past, and yet dwelling in the past can of course prevent us from being able to heal and move forward. Both of these suggested activities, futures visioning and gathering oral histories, especially when implemented together, can provide teachers with a means of helping students address the past and therefore move towards a more just and peaceful future. At the same time, when engaging in these two activities, students are also being exposed to other versions of the past, and are in conversation with diverse others about what a less violent future together might look like. This is essential for a variety of reasons and yet occurs in only the rarest of classrooms. First, it is entirely possible that a critical peace educator's classroom is the only place in which a young person from a non-hegemonic culture encounters a narrative that represents them with dignity (or indeed, that represents them at all). It also may well be the only site where students from dominant cultures hear narratives of the conflict other than their own.

In addition, a critical peace educator who offers her students the opportunity to envision a future of just coexistence in an egalitarian, safe and democratic space, in my view, contributes to a larger and necessary process of narrative transformation. Peace building is necessarily a multi-track process (Diamond and McDonald 1996), and schools inevitably are limited in their ability to build peace—as are any other sectors that are a part of the overall peace system. But schools and curriculum are essential to the peace building process, I would argue, and especially to the sorts of violent, complex and entrenched conflicts involving a potent mix of historical trauma,

# Peace Education, Chosen Traumas and Collective Memory    31

nationalism, religion, and ethnic identity. Such conflicts require narrative transformation and large-scale trauma healing, among other tools of conflict resolution, to interrupt the cycle of revenge and trans-generational trauma. Along with political leadership, policy and institutional reform, and addressing media narratives of the conflict, both curriculum and pedagogy must be an aspect of any comprehensive effort to build sustainable peace. The conflict of which 9/11 is a manifestation is no exception.

Peace educators are increasingly aware of the need to address collective memory and historical narratives in their teaching. A recent work in this vein is Beckerman and Zembylas's *Teaching Contested Narratives* (2012). I believe this will prove to be a foundational work for the intersection of the literature on historical memory and the literature on peace education. They challenge peace educators to consider the fundamental epistemologies underlying much Western peace education. They question the assumption that the values of peace education (at least as commonly presented by Western writers such as myself) are indeed universal: "We believe that when peace (education) is presented as a universal utopia, this stops its potential productivity by representing its values as universally self-evident" (Beckerman and Zembylas 2012, p. 27). Such an approach glosses over the realities of power and hegemony, as critical peace educators have been arguing for some time now. The trouble as they frame it is that "In the Western tradition, differences need to be first pointed out and then assimilated or destroyed . . . and what is more important, differences are set in the realm of meaning and not in the realm of *power relations*" (Beckerman and Zembylas 2012, p. 27, emphasis theirs). Zembylas and Beckerman are hardly alone in this observation, as they note. Narrative conflict resolutionists have been addressing just this (Winslade and Monk 2008, Cobb 2013) by employing narrative conflict resolution practices to make heard previously silenced peoples or histories. Bajaj writes about the importance of illuminating the workings of power in her study on human rights education in India (2013). Cole's edition, *Teaching the Violent Past*, offers powerful case studies from post-conflict countries regarding how teachers and curriculum writers have struggled to tell an accurate and diverse story regarding the genocides or civil wars they have endured. I have written on implementing CPE in a juvenile detention home; a focus of our curriculum was power dynamics in the local community (Duckworth 2011). Critical peace educators have been having this conversation for some time now; why then has more progress not been made? Simply put, schools are of the state. They are government institutions subject to politics (as most of the teachers I interviewed were quite aware) and related restrictions on what teachers must and must not cover. Critical peace education emphasizes identifying these narrative silences and asking how they came to be and why they persist.

Beckerman and Zembylas continue on to focus on two other habits of Western epistemology. One is the tendency still with us from the age of positivism to frame all of reality as either/or binaries. The second, related, habit

32    *9/11 and Collective Memory in U.S. Classrooms*

is demonization "of those who are not like us" (Beckerman and Zembylas, 2013, p. 27). This allows too much Western thought to ignore "complex historical processes which have brought the West, the colonial powers of old, to successfully replace the force of arms with the force of homogenization" (Beckerman and Zembylas, 2013, p. 27). Given how immediately this relates to current grievances throughout the "Arab World", with particular regard to Western funding of autocratic and oppressive regimes, helping students to understand just these complex historical processes is vital to a quality education regarding 9/11. I am defining "quality" here as an education that will empower students to be informed, active and critical citizens.

Beckerman and Zembylas further draw on their experiences teaching in their native Israel (Beckerman) and Greece (Zembylas) to share data suggesting just how difficult it is for even those who wish for peace to relate to "the other" in ways that are equitable and trusting enough to perhaps lead to some sort of reconciliation. Their study is an important reminder that teachers themselves, of course, are impacted by the conflicts in their communities and have all of the complex identities that anyone else has; we must prioritize their healing and personal and professional development if we can expect them to play a leading role in building sustainable peace. For example, they relate the story of a series of dialogues they hosted (each in his own home country) for teachers wishing to bring peace and reconciliation pedagogy into their classrooms. Even these teachers—the "choir" we often preach to, if you will—were amazed at how difficult the work of dialogue in the context of a protracted social conflict truly was. Teachers cannot be asked to undertake such work without support, and school systems likewise cannot be asked to undertake peace building without community and policy support. I emphasize this point because of the tendency I observe in the U.S. to view our schools in isolation from their communities, while we simultaneously turn to them for solutions to all manner of social ills. Their call for teachers and school systems to utterly transform not just methodology but epistemology—the assumptions we make about what constitutes knowledge itself and who gets to say what "counts" as knowledge—is compelling. It also informs my own exploration of how 9/11 is being taught and what this in turn suggests for our ability to transform the current conflict between the U.S. and the "Islamic World".

## RESTORYING: TRANSFORMATIVE
## NARRATIVES AND PEACE EDUCATION

As the field of conflict resolution continues its evolution, scholars and practitioners increasingly attend to peacebuilding and reconciliation that will prove durable and sustainable (Schirch 2005, Lederach 2005, Ramsbotham et al. 2011). For example, will a particular process of peace building be able to withstand setbacks that might occur due to the violence of spoilers? Will

*Peace Education, Chosen Traumas and Collective Memory* 33

the negotiated cease fire hold? If it does, are the conflict parties in danger of reigniting the conflict in the years following? The literature on the role of historical memory in peace-building and conflict resolution tends to observe that absent narrative transformation, the roots of protracted social conflicts have probably not been addressed. Sara Cobb, for example, writes that, " . . . narrative analysis emerges as an important research method for attending to meaning- making processes, power dynamics, and parties' language-in-use, in a specific conflict context. Narrative analysis provides a *diagnostic* framework for understanding conflict that has direct import for conflict intervention" (in Cheldelin 2003, p. 101).

This approach to building peace falls within the larger framework of what I have previously called "systemic conflict resolution" (Duckworth, 2011), which addresses the macro-historical processes, systems and institutions which may well be driving a conflict (Rubenstein 2008, Jeong 2000, Tidwell 2001). Systemic conflict resolution typically investigates dynamics of power and inequality which might have driven the conflict. It focuses on the role of policies and institutions, which may have been a factor in fostering any relevant perceived injustices and works with all stakeholders to creatively transform those policies and institutions such that the conflict is far less likely to reoccur (Jeong 2000, Ramsbotham, et al. 2011). Hegemonic narratives (Galtung, 1990) can function as a means of structural violence just as surely as economic or political systems. Such narratives, in fact, often serve precisely to legitimize inequitable or oppressive political or economic systems. They tend to position the in-group as an innocent victim, and the out-group as the aggressor who has not at all been victimized. To the extent that the out-group has suffered, according to such narratives, they have deserved it for past actions. These conflict narratives, as I call them, work to delegitimize the Other, or in more extreme examples, to quite literally render them invisible. For example, officials in Soviet Russia once undertook explicit efforts to erase from any records or memory the reality of a town's famine (Khubova et al. 2005, pp. 89–102). For this reason, approaches to peace education increasingly involve students in perceiving, analyzing and deconstructing these collective conflict narratives. They also, hopefully, engage students in together creating a new narrative of peaceful and cooperative co-existence.

This emphasis on the macro-systemic underlying causes of violent conflict (and hence trauma) has lead a number of us to view the role of collective memory, and history more broadly, in conflict resolution as essential to peace processes that are truly capable of addressing a conflict at its roots (Lederach 2005, Korostelina 2011, Tidwell 2001; Hart 2008). Any policy, institution or conflict has an historical context, and the field of conflict resolution has made some real progress recently with respect to understanding the role of history in conflict perpetuation and resolution. Narrative transformation is one central contribution (Cobb 2013), stemming from the insight of many peace and conflict scholars that, as important as group

34  *9/11 and Collective Memory in U.S. Classrooms*

processes and communication skills might indeed be to facilitating resolution, often much larger historical forces are at work in a conflict (Cobb 2003). Faced with such "protracted social conflicts" (Azar 1990), our classic conflict resolution tools of mediation, negotiation and facilitation may prove insufficient in the absence of policy, institutional or even socio-cultural transformation. While we hear this point made commonly, arguably our conflict resolution practice tools have not kept up with our theories and concepts. This is particularly true if said mediated or facilitated dialogues fail to grapple with the weight of the history driving and shaping the worldviews, material contexts, needs and identities of the parties to the conflict. In such cases history seems to act as a weight pressing on the conflict parties or a maze through which a peace worker must find her way. She must ask a number of complex questions. How do the conflict groups understand themselves and their role in the world, the cosmos? What cultural myths and metaphors are relevant? Are they deployed in the narratives the group tells itself about the protracted conflict? What role has the conflict, and particular events within it, had in shaping or reshaping the group's identity? All of these questions are relevant to genuine peacebuilding and form what I call a conflict group's "narrative motivation". Narrative motivation again is the underlying cultural story, grounded in a group's identity and history that constitutes how they explain who they are in the cosmos and relatedly, why they have behaved as they have in regards to the conflict. This narrative motivation must be addressed, and the underlying needs met, if a conflict is to be truly resolved. By investigating how 9/11 is being taught, I hope of course to understand more about the narrative Americans are telling ourselves about 9/11. What was our narrative motivation for our response? What narrative motivation, if there is a coherent one, explains the behavior of the U.S. (and allies) and Islamic extremists towards each other throughout the past several decades? After all, 9/11 was not the beginning of this conflict. It was an *event* in a wider conflict.

As Lederach (2005) and others have noted, we cannot address such protracted conflicts without attempting reconciliation, which to my mind precisely means wrestling with the weight of that history. Lederach writes that our collective stories are what weave us into the social web (to use his metaphor) of society, culture, history and time. Our collective narrative tells us who, why and what we are (Lederach 2005, p. 140–145). Chosen traumas then represent a rupture in the ability of a people to tell and be connected to their Story. Violence "might best be understood as the disruption—and far too often the outright destruction—of a people's story" (Lederach 2005, p. 138). Hence, Lederach argues, we must "re-story". This concept of "re-story" strikes me as workably similar to narrative transformation and is essential for peace educators engaging narratives of historical trauma in the classroom. To re-story is to re-empower a people to speak for and define themselves. To re-story is to facilitate healing from the wounds of history. This will necessitate social and political transformation.

# Peace Education, Chosen Traumas and Collective Memory 35

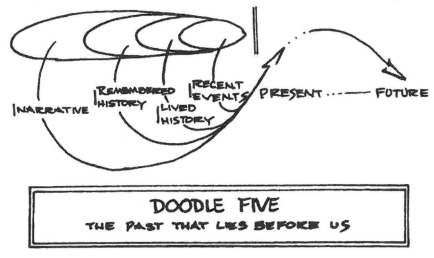

Figure 2.1  Model: Lederach 2005, p. 141.

Certainly the tools of facilitation, mediation and negotiation are a part of this process, but the process of building peace is much deeper, more difficult and much more long-term. Lederach refers to this as understanding "the past that lies before us", that is, the history that shapes who we are and the legacies we inherit. I place this study fully in this growing school of conflict resolution which insists that without confronting the wounds and injustices of history, we cannot expect to build peace. The past is not over, as Faulkner once wrote, it's not even past. Certainly security, intelligence, traditional Track 1 diplomacy, political reform and economic development are all important to intervening in the global conflict between the U.S. and the Islamic World. Yet without addressing the long term narratives at play, I do not believe those interventions on their own will prove sufficient.

9/11 certainly was such an injustice, and our field is uniquely positioned to help the public understand how this has impacted the psyche of the nation and what the implications for future dynamics of peace and conflict might be. Extrapolating from the graphic above, the collective narrative about 9/11 will certainly be grounded in both remembered and lived history. It will also be grounded in the narrative, to include relevant emotions, symbols and metaphors, of the perceived U.S. relationship with the Muslim World in general. Given how that fraught history has driven and continues to drive violent conflict globally, the urgency of "re-storying" becomes clear. Understanding how 9/11 is being taught is an essential part of this "re-storying". As Volkan (1998) noted, when a society has not allowed itself to grieve and heal from a great historical loss or trauma, again, the pain and rage often entraps parties in a cycle of revenge and violence, and of course the mechanism of trans-generational trauma suggests the likelihood of the

## 36    9/11 and Collective Memory in U.S. Classrooms

entrapment of future generations as well, unless the cycle is interrupted. Reconciliation would then be impossible. As the above suggests, the field of peace and conflict studies is producing some promising working regarding the relevance of collective memory to conflict resolution. Yet there has not yet been an exploration of 9/11 as a chosen trauma, or a full study of how 9/11 is being taught, and what the implications of this are for potential narrative conflict resolution.


## CRITICAL EMOTIONAL PRAXIS

One other important intersection between the literature on historical memory and the literature on peace education is Zembylas's concept of *critical emotional praxis* (Zembylas 2008, Beckerman and Zembylas 2012). In his words, critical emotional praxis "creates openings for different affective relations with others". The point here "is to explore the conditions under which trauma impacts educators' and students' lives, to destabilize and denaturalize that regime of thought that perpetuates a conflicting ethos with those who are deemed responsible for 'our' trauma, and to invent new practices of relating to others". For this to be achieved, what he calls "dangerous memories" (2008, pp. 133–157) must be allowed to come to the fore. Trauma obviously creates pain and suffering, around which we as humans naturally desire to create meaning. We also desire to restore physical, mental, emotional and even I would argue *cultural* security. In seeking to achieve both of these goals, we often harden the boundaries between "us" and "them", them being of course the groups we have identified as the perpetrators. For teachers, this means being aware of the spaces of inclusion and exclusion in our classrooms. Trauma narratives often privilege the narrative of those positioned as the victim, and marginalize and silence those seen as the perpetrators.

In the case of the historical trauma of 9/11, dangerous memories might include memories of Muslim students, immigrants, or other similarly marginalized students in the wake of 9/11. The 1953 CIA coup in Tehran is another appropriate example, as are U.S. military bases in Saudi Arabia and the ongoing conflict between Israel and Palestine. Memories of FDNY firefighters who did not have working radio equipment should not be censored. Stories of Afghan civilians struggling to survive the Soviet invasion, the Taliban regime and the U.S. invasion after 9/11 must be given air. Surfacing and creating space in the classroom for such dangerous memories is essential for students "to understand how trauma operates through affective connections and articulates its differences from other places around the world" (Zembylas, 2008, p. 5). Such pedagogy "develops capacities for critical emotional praxis" which can inspire and strengthen the skills needed for peace building. Zembylas refers to this as the "pedagogy of dangerous memories" (Zembylas with Beckerman, 2008, pp. 133–156). As we

## Peace Education, Chosen Traumas and Collective Memory 37

will see in Chapters 3–5, many classroom teachers find it difficult enough simply to find time to address 9/11 at all, given the demands of state centralized curriculum. Thus it is hard to imagine critical emotional praxis or discussions around 'dangerous memories' taking place on any regular enough basis to disrupt harmful orthodox national narratives about 9/11. Rather dramatic changes in school structure and policy would be necessary. That said, as we will see more in Chapter 4, there are teachers finding subversive and creative ways to at least complicate the narrative of 9/11 somewhat and to humanize the Other.

## RECONCILIATION PEDAGOGY

Reconciliation pedagogy (RP), a manifestation in some ways of CPE, has been a central theme and objective of peace educators. Some insights from the literature on this are useful here. RP typically engages students in learning and dialogues about particularly traumatic, contested or painful history. Yet it does not stop there; the aim is to inspire in students the desire, and to nurture the skills necessary for, increasing social justice. This has been wildly controversial as it has often been misperceived as asking the grandchildren "to carry a burden of guilt for what their parents and grandparents have done". Such approaches, as one reflection on South Africa's TRC observed, "are notoriously unsuccessful, and for good reason" (Christie in Ahluwalia, 2012, p. 42). Still, "it is an appropriate pedagogical goal to teach students about thoughtful engagement with the responsibilities of public life" (ibid). While some of the critiques are overstated, certainly reconciliation pedagogy must be handled with skill by an experienced and trusted facilitator. The facilitator of such historical dialogues must be able to provide nuanced context, navigate the divergent views that will certainly be in her classroom and at least try to bracket her own feelings about the historical conflict. As I have been emphasizing, teachers do not shed their politics or identities while in front of the classroom.

There is wisdom here for those wishing to address 9/11 in a comprehensive manner: implications, not accusation! Nor will such an approach involve teachers having to tell students "what to think". Rather, reconciliation pedagogy is important for basic citizenship education in societies that have been divided or that have suffered serious historical trauma. As Christie writes, "This is not about politicization, or making simple judgments of right and wrong in terms of pre-existing moral codes. Rather it is about building our own and our students' understanding of the ways in which the public realm is constituted and maintained. . . . It is about cultivating an awareness that the public realm is precarious, and that it is built, and eroded, in the mundane and everyday activities of ordinary people. . . ." (Christie in Ahluwalia 2012, p. 43). Thus teachers, from this starting point, can (and on occasion do) engage students in conversations relating the

## 38  9/11 and Collective Memory in U.S. Classrooms

violence of 9/11 to school violence, bullying (especially of Muslim students) and the ethical implications of being a bystander. As Crowley suggests, young people have distinct political voices and needs, and their potential for fostering real change should not be overlooked (Crowley in Ahluwalia 2012, pp. 93–117). She does also raise an interesting point regarding the impact of peace or reconciliation pedagogy in a classroom of students "whose first-hand knowledge of war and genocide is entirely media-shaped and experienced through a production process that filters into television and web-surfing lives". This meant that "questions of who is the subject and object of reconciliation pedagogy become critical" (Crowley in Ahluwalia 2012 pg. 103). The implications for teaching about 9/11 seem significant, and some of my responding teachers did grapple with them. The teachers who accomplished this did so primarily by working to destabilize and complicate harmful stereotypes of Muslims, by trying to place 9/11 in historical context and by complicating the definition of that fraught word "terrorist". I would argue that any "reconciliation pedagogy" regarding the conflict between the U.S. and "the Muslim World", of which 9/11 is a manifestation, must include historical grievances that relevant countries have against the U.S. (such as drone strikes and military aid to oppressive regimes) and vice versa. Again, one need not "tell students what to think" to introduce such a "history from the point of view of the Other" (following Zinn) and allow students to dig into such complexities.

## REALIZING PRAXIS FOR AN END TO WAR: EMPOWERING ACTION FOR PEACE

Another critique or challenge of peace education is worth considering here. Ultimately critical peace educators wish to do more than just inspire critical thinking about power inequalities or the legacies of historical injustice. We wish to inspire informed action—the essence of praxis. Praxis, as many of my readers will know, has been a central concept of thinking about peace, conflict and education since Paolo Freire himself (2003). Maria Montessori, at least in my reading of her, can also be seen in this vein, as she called for development of a "new man" (Montessori 1949) through an utterly transformed kind of education. This kind of education would, as those familiar with Montessori schools will know, eschew centralized, narrowly quantitative standards to focus on developing each individual child's creative and critical capacities, as well as his social and emotional capacities. Montessori's theory was that this new sort of education was needed if mankind were to finally end the devastation of war. Her view was that war, at least in some sense, occurred because human beings lacked the capacity to resolve conflicts nonviolently. She of course believed, as I do, that education is one key sector in developing such creative, critical and empathic capacities (Montessori 1949). She argued that the form of education that we currently

## Peace Education, Chosen Traumas and Collective Memory    39

practice, based as it is on students having to compete with other students, socializes young people for war. As she writes, "The failure, the weakling, the slave, and the arrested personality are, in short, always the products of an education that is a blind struggle between the strong and the weak" (p. 19). This developed in students a culture of exclusion and hierarchy, even aggression, towards others, especially those constructed as different or inferior in a particular historical narrative (as Muslims and Arabs too often are today). Montessori (1949) continues, "The most rewarded and most encouraged virtue has been besting his classmates and coming out on top. . . . Men educated in this manner have not been prepared to seek truth . . . nor to be charitable towards others and to cooperate with them to create a better life for all. . . . On the contrary, the education they have received has prepared them for . . . war. For the truth of the matter is that war is caused not by arms but by man" (p. 21).

Educators of course have long known that the values children are socialized with have implications for the health of a society, but Montessori was a visionary in her linking of the organization and priorities of early schooling to war. A child socialized to compete will be prepared in his consciousness as an adult to conquer. Empathy, collaboration and cooperation ought to be the values that inform schooling. Montessori (1949) speaks of universality as a central value and urges its teaching as a means of education aiding in the prevention of war:

> The young person is urged to study, to buckle down, to conserve his time, to get ahead in the world. Poor thing. When he has completed his studies, he knows nothing of social life, and he feels lost and forsaken. . . . I will simply say that as we see it, man must be inspired to seek universality until the day he dies. Man thus prepared, conscious of his mission in the cosmos, will be capable of building the new world of peace. (p. 83)

Present day peace educators often note that today's travel and communications technologies make the development of this sort of global consciousness possible (even as our weapons technologies make it increasingly more urgent). From my interdisciplinary standpoint, I would note that even the most peaceful schools alone are not likely to be able to prevent a particular war, as she herself implied. Political and economic leadership are essential. And yet how are we to develop the leaders and institutions that we need to prevent war without attention to education?

Similarly, Freire (2003) argued that education ought to be centered around curriculum that spoke directly to urgent and felt problems in a community's shared life. He argued that oppressed communities were not always aware of the systems of power and privilege that oppressed them. A key role of education then for him was to achieve such awareness—what he called critical consciousness. This new awareness would lay the intellectual

## 40   *9/11 and Collective Memory in U.S. Classrooms*

and social groundwork for praxis. He wrote seminally of the ways in which marginalized peoples can internalize the historical narratives and cultural identity of the dominant group; as he writes, this prevents them (us) from being able to name and thus have agency in the world. While at first blush this may sound insignificant, lacking access to such social dialogue processes historically has prevented marginalized groups from being able to reproduce their culture and meet their basic human needs. By naming the world, I read him to mean participation in describing, and therefore shaping, it. This is 'naming' in an almost Edenic sense of the word, as Adam and Eve named creation as a manifestation of their agency. As he puts it, "Two subjects meet to name the world in order to transform it" (Freire, 2003, p. 167). If both parties involved are subjects, they are both of equal power. Developing critical awareness in students (and teachers) makes dialogue essential for a classroom. CPE educators often, rightly in my view, critique the status quo approach to education as monologue, rather than dialogue. Freire famously called this the "banking" model of education and decried it as a tool of oppression (2003, p. 73). *Pedagogy of the Oppressed* called for education based in dialogue and critical inquiry into themes that are felt by students to be important to the reality of their lives. Applying this to what we'll learn below about how 9/11 is being taught, we can see that historical silences—what is not taught—can be seen as a form of monologue. Too often 9/11 is not addressed at all, or addressed only in a rather thin, ahistorical and decontextualized manner, as we'll see teachers describing below. Indeed, a desire to engage students in critical historical dialogue emerged clearly in my data. As some of my participating teachers argue, students need and deserve an opportunity to "name" 9/11 in the Freirian sense—to fully understand the 9/11 era, and form their opinions through engaged critical reflection.

What unites these two cornerstone theorists of peace education is the notion that education was capable of producing people with the capacities to solve the greatest human challenges. For Freire, this was the horrors of the military junta in Brazil and how education for liberation could inspire resistance and demands for justice and freedom. For Montessori, looking at history through the smoke and char of WWII, and with the advent of the age of WMD, the urgency to bring an end to war was real. Montessori was one of the first theorists to call for child-led learning, explicitly linking it to a culture of peace (1949).

So we can see that education has long been thought of as a means of attempting to intervene in larger social and political processes. Scholars and practitioners have since their work built on Montessori and Freire, trying to work out locally appropriate and concrete ways to manifest their vision. Despite the depth of my admiration for these two seminal thinkers, I take a more circumspect and limited view here. As critical to personal and national development as education obviously is, my own view is somewhat closer to Beckerman and Zembylas. There are simply limits to the role schools can play in impacting conflict systems, and I repeat this explicitly even as I argue that at the same time, we must not neglect the role schooling plays, for good or ill, in peace and conflict systems. Peace building is a multi-track process.

Given these limits, how do we achieve peace praxis in a particular classroom? How do we inspire action around a particular issue? This has been a question occupying the CPE literature for decades now, and there is not space for a full exploration of this literature. I have written on the model I developed elaborating how CPE can be maximized for social change elsewhere; to quickly summarize here, CPE can at its best can foster a sense of dignity (of both self and other). This in turn can provide fertile ground for latent social movements as marginalized groups learn to articulate shared grievances. As these social movements grow and collaborate, opportunity develops for a global civil society to emerge. This then can facilitate conflict transformation, as global civil society works to address the types of structural violence that so often drive conflict (Duckworth in Duckworth and Kelley, 2013, pp. 50–72). I readily acknowledge the chain of logic I describe above is an ideal, though I do think it provides a conceptually useful map for what we as critical peace educators hope to achieve.

Two key principles I think can guide development of such curriculum. The first would be to connect schools to their communities. Partnerships with local non-profits who are working to address community challenges can provide students a real-world means of developing the critical and creative capacities needed for both democratic citizenship and peace building. Youth Radio, a project of NPR that features youth voices on issues of urgency to them, is one example. Amnesty International Morocco works with high schools around Rabat to engage students in awareness and activism around human rights (though this was limited by the political context which can view challenges to the monarchy with suspicion).

In another discussion of CPE, I describe a project in which educators involved their students in a multi-disciplinary, experiential curriculum around Hurricane Katrina as combined social studies, environmental science, history and language arts curriculum. They were able to speak with survivors and interrogate the racial inequalities of public policy around emergency relief. Students moved towards praxis when they engaged lawmakers regarding unkept promises to Katrina survivors (Duckworth 2011). Another example of an effective school-community partnership involved a local non-profit dedicated to arts for peace in schools. Local teachers worked with this group to develop a project in which students wrote and performed an original musical that explored themes of bullying and school violence (Duckworth, Williams and Allen 2012). This example in particular, while powerful and beneficial for students, especially demonstrated one of the most significant challenges for such partnerships: resources. Ultimately the peace theatre project may not prove sustainable unless continued funding is allocated, something policy makers have found exceedingly

42    *9/11 and Collective Memory in U.S. Classrooms*

hard in the current economic and political environment. Time of course is another key resource; as our analysis noted, teachers and students alike, despite their passion for the project, struggled sometimes to find time for planning, rehearsal and the numerous other tasks involved in any theatre production. The teachers involved in particular were not relieved of any other duties to accommodate taking this project on (Duckworth, Williams and Allen 2012).

Despite the challenges, these sorts of partnerships can help students in critical peace education classrooms move from critical reflection to effective action. In the case of the conflict between the U.S. and the Muslim World, students can be engaged in interfaith dialogues. Local universities and houses of worship would be perfect partners for such engagement. As the teachers I interviewed will observe frequently in Chapters 3–5, the key will be to change the current cultural mindset about education such that experiential activities and critical thinking are not seen as peripheral by policy makers.

Student leadership to the greatest extent possible is a second important principle of effective CPE. This emerges clearly from some of the examples of school-community partnerships described above. Students were not only invited to study and speak out on issues impacting them, they were invited to engage with policy makers or with public audiences. Little else can replace these sorts of experiences for helping students to internalize not just the skills we want them to learn, but what those skills are for. CPE proponents like myself have long been arguing that this kind of experiential, community based and interdisciplinary curriculum is urgently needed.

This brings our brief tour of the literature on peace education and historical memory to a topic not frequently enough explored, to my mind: authentic assessment. While not frequently on the radar screens of educational philosophers writing about historical memory in the classroom, I contend that the means we use to assess students represent a real barrier in teachers' minds to the in-depth, relevant and experiential work they would like to have students doing. We will see this theme emerge in Ch. 4 especially. If teacher and student performance is solely measured by scantron tests that professional educators often have little involvement in creating, we can readily see how difficult it would be dedicate significant time to the sorts of community-school partnerships and historical dialogues I describe above. The question of authentic assessment in the context of CPE is underexplored and assessment in my view remains too anecdotal. Specifically we need to further develop creative means of evaluating CPE. There is not space here for a full review of the literature on assessment, which could fill its own book. Still in my observation, we tend to spend more time elaborating the problems with the status quo as opposed to developing alternatives that would work for CPE specifically. Critical pedagogues have long made the link between rote memorization, standardization and war, but not necessarily in the context of teaching historical dialogues. I'd like to make that

## Peace Education, Chosen Traumas and Collective Memory   43

link explicit here. Teaching contested traumatic history represents an even more challenging context, needless to say, than the average classroom faces but this makes authentic assessment even more necessary. In the context of, say, writing, advocates of authentic assessment might recommend that instead of a grammar sheet, students must be asked to write! But what happens when we want to assess relational skills, the ability to resolve conflict, or empathy? What about prejudice reduction? We need more narrative, humanistic and qualitative means of assessing these sorts of objectives. These abilities relate directly to our goals as critical peace educators, especially when we bring traumatic and contested history into our classrooms.

One possible way forward would be to think along the lines of qualitative criteria not just for assessing individual students and teachers, but for evaluating an overall school culture of peace. This has been an important theme of the literature on peace education, especially in cases where school leaders are working to address the impacts of socio-historical conflicts in their hallways. The need for such emerged clearly in my data, as I'll discuss in Chapters 3–5. I offer the below criteria as one means of approaching the evaluation of a school's peaceable culture.

1. Is the school multi-lingual? This becomes especially important when historical divides have been ethno-national. The conflict groups will almost certainly speak different languages and demand that their mother tongue be represented in schools and elsewhere.
2. Do students have a voice in shaping the school rules or norms? In particular, are there identifiable means of inclusion of the voices of students who might otherwise be marginalized?
3. Is there an observable culture of community service and activism?
4. Is there a culture of "classrooms without walls" through which students can be involved in meaningful projects that improve their communities?
5. Does the school offer interdisciplinary, experiential curriculum, ideally grounded in themes of and questions regarding peace and conflict?

Such questions are not well suited to the common quantitative types of assessment; given that the focus is school culture, ethnography seems an ideal methodology for investigating some of the above possible indicators.

### THE LIMITS OF PEACE EDUCATION

Finally, peace educators, and the literature on the role of schools in peace and conflict, have recently been grappling with the limits of CPE. Lynn Davies is prominent among the scholars researching the limits of, as she calls it, education against extremism (Davies 2008). She has also explored

## 44  *9/11 and Collective Memory in U.S. Classrooms*

the mirror image of peace education, war education, which is to say the ways in which education too often reproduces the dynamics that give rise to conflict. This is a potentiality peace educators must obviously be aware of. She argues that textbooks and teachers too often reproduce stereotypes in schools. As Davis (2008) notes, an important insight of the literature on peace education and historical memory is the way in which textbooks tend to codify and institutionalize the narrative of the victors (p. 140). As noted above, other analysts have focused on this as well (Korostelina 2008, Cole 2007). Korostelina (2008) detailed the often thin and one-sided narratives of WWII in Korean, Chinese, Irish and Taiwanese textbooks. Cole especially detailed the difficulties of trying to write the history books on what exactly happened in countries like El Salvador, Honduras and Guatemala during those conflicts. She finds that the textbooks ultimately were not able to fully explore the terrible truths of torture, disappearances, rape and other brutalities that occurred. Looking to address such problems, Israeli and Palestinian educators have worked to integrate schools and used innovations such as jointly written texts and bilingual education in both Hebrew and Arabic.

Even further, Davies explores the way in which some schools discipline, and which can socialize young citizens for a kind of unthinking identification with authority that threatens democracy. I suggested above that the development of processes to involve students in creating school rules and norms is an important indicator of a school culture of peace. Davies seems to have in mind something similar here. She strongly critiques the manner in which many schools approach discipline, based in hierarchy and monologue, not dialogue, and links it to what she calls "war education" (2004, pp. 109–123). She concludes her discussion of 'war education' observing that education has contributed to a culture of violence and fear via the

> fatal combination of greed (for superiority) and fear (of failure). . . . A fearful population is easily mobilized for war. . . . Politicians play on people's fears and through examinations teachers play children's fears; both of these dynamics contribute to threat inflation. . . . Whether formally preparing young people to accept and engage in war, conflict and violence, whether by informal brutality, whether by regimes of fear, testing competition or by simply remaining silent or ineffectual about violence, educational institutions are directly culpable in the reproduction of conflict. (2004, p. 123)

Thus some of our work as critical peace educators is creating what we want to see going on in classrooms, and some of it remains transforming what we know will reproduce cultures of violence and war. As regards 'educating against extremism' in particular, with its clear relevance to my own study of teaching 9/11, Davies argues for what she calls hybridity, fostering a culture in worldwide classrooms that helps students to be comfortable with multiple truths and different ways of being (2008, pp. 33–34). She notes that extremism is rooted in ideologies of exclusion that precisely refuse any sort of hybridity. Only curriculum and methodologies that invite students to discern, explore and act in multi-cultural contexts can develop this sort of worldview. It is a vital attitude for functioning in the 21st century.

## WHY SCHOOLS?

There is wide consensus among peace educators and scholars of peace and conflict resolution that schools are essential to collective identity and to processes of peace building—and perpetuating conflict (Duckworth 2011, Duckworth in Duckworth and Kelley, eds, 2012, Bajaj 2008, Bajaj 2012, Beckerman and Zembylas 2012, Davies 2004, McGlynn et al. 2009, Cole 2008). As instruments of the state, schools and formal curriculum often propagate the government's own view of a particular historical conflict, which needless to say is only one view point and is quite likely contested, even if such dissent has successfully been silenced (Cole 2008). Societies also often look to school systems to teach values such as loyalty and patriotism and to transmit the national narratives that form the basis of how a country has come to imagine itself as a community (Anderson 1991). Along with families, the media, community and/or faith institutions, and state institutions such as museums, schools and curriculum are instrumental to shaping the content and contours of a nation's collective understanding of its identity, and especially its memory of significant events. Nowhere is this truer than how a nation remembers war and conflict.

How then are the events of Sept. 11, 2001, being taught in America's middle and high school classrooms? This is the central question of this book. Eleven years after the attacks, much literature has been dedicated to the importance of teaching about the attacks on the U.S., often exhorting teachers to properly instill patriotic pride or charging them to 'never forget'. Critical pedagogues like me worry that the sort of patriotism often emphasized by state curriculum enforces obedience and unquestioning loyalty over thoughtful engagement and critical thinking (Davies 2004, Giroux 2011, McLaren and Kincheloe 2007, Westheimer 2007). Scholars have written volumes of advice for teachers on how they ought to be teaching such a monumental event, developing curriculum for teachers, and educators have published personal reflections (primarily from college and university professors, but some from middle and high school teachers as well) on their own classroom experiences regarding teaching 9/11. As one may imagine, this is especially true of teachers whose classrooms were impacted in some particular way by the attacks. But we still need to know what teachers are actually doing in the classroom. We currently have no such overall portrait. Are teachers making use of all of this advice and curriculum? What sort of activities do they undertake? How do they go about deciding what they

## 46  9/11 and Collective Memory in U.S. Classrooms

will do? How do they assess its impact? What sort of barriers do they face when teaching about 9/11, be they emotional, bureaucratic or political? How do they feel about teaching such a painful and almost unavoidably political subject, especially given that what we might call the post-9/11 era has been so partisan and so divided precisely with respect to related issues such as the invasions of Iraq and Afghanistan, Guantanamo Bay and the use of torture during interrogations.

I have investigated the above questions by speaking directly to middle and high school teachers, via both quantitative questionnaire and qualitative interviews, to create a more broad and comprehensive picture than has yet been painted of how 9/11 is being taught to today's middle and high school students. While the current literature, especially that by professors and teachers themselves reflecting on their own experiences of teaching 9/11, gives us a sense of what those particular teachers are thinking and feeling about teaching this subject, to date these "dots" have not yet been truly connected. We have much curriculum available for teacher use, we have textbook analysis (e.g. Hess and Stoddard 2007, 2011), and we have a set of personal reflections on teaching 9/11, but we still need a comprehensive sense of how and how much (if at all) 9/11 is being taught. Given the terrible import of that day, the understanding the first "post 9/11 generation" has of what happened and what it means is significant to how Americans will view foreign policy in the coming decades, especially foreign policy as regards the Islamic World. This is what makes understanding how 9/11 is being taught so urgent. In light of the above, this study addresses two compelling questions not yet addressed in the literature.

1. How (if at all) is 9/11 being taught in U.S. classrooms? What coherent narrative, if any, is being passed on to todays' middle and high school students about that day and what it means?
2. What are the implications of the above for the future trajectory of this conflict, especially as regards potential for narrative conflict resolution?

Again, such understanding is especially key since, in my view, 9/11, and the wars in Afghanistan and Iraq (as well as drone strike unofficial escalations in places such as Yemen, Somalia and Pakistan) are all events in one wider conflict between the U.S. and predominantly Muslim nations. If I am correct that 9/11 has become a chosen trauma for the U.S., peace researchers must be able to make use of this knowledge by designing appropriate narrative transformation interventions. We cannot hope to begin this without a deeper and more empirical knowledge of the "trauma narrative" itself than we currently have. As Sturken aptly wrote, "the way a nation remembers a war and constructs its history is directly related to how that nation further propagates war" (1997, p. 122). Peace education that addresses historical memory and trauma can be an ideal intervention.

# 3 Inside the Classroom

The centerpiece of this book is the classroom and the experiences, feelings and perceptions of our teachers. Here I will share the results of my quantitative data, gathered from a nationwide survey of teachers grades 6–12. (I did not include elementary school teachers on the grounds that the subject of 9/11 is likely too difficult for younger students, but this could arguably be useful as a future study.) I asked teachers how often they broached the subject of 9/11, what sort of activities in particular they implement, if they used any published curriculum, if they felt "safe" addressing such a controversial and painful topic, and whether they felt they had experienced any barriers to teaching about 9/11. (See Appendix A for Survey.)

Before unveiling the results, we need some details about how the study was conducted. This was a nationwide survey of public school teachers (some of which were charter schools), grades 6–12. I conducted the survey online to ensure teacher ease of response and to better offer participants anonymity. This survey asked ten questions about how teachers approached teaching 9//11—or why they did not do so. In the objective survey, teachers could elaborate in the comment box. 150 valid respondents participated. We did have to eliminate some responses, such as those which were from guidance counselors or from non-U.S. teachers. I recruited from my own personal network of educators, as well as from teacher professional organizations. Prior to putting the survey in the field, I pilot-tested the survey questions with a group of colleagues who are currently high school teachers. Their feedback helped me to clarify the wording of my questions.

By and large, 9/11 is not being addressed in any substantive manner in the classroom. 23% of my survey participants report that they do not address 9/11 at all!

A majority of the teachers—65%—who do not address 9/11 reported that this is because they do not perceive it to be a part of their curriculum. The study was open to all teachers, not just social studies or English, so this may account for some of this perception. Still, as some of the teachers I spoke with during interviews elaborated, one can address the events of 9/11 from the perspective of any discipline. Ideally, in fact, a unit on 9/11 would be interdisciplinary, involving of course history and social studies, but also literature,

48   9/11 and Collective Memory in U.S. Classrooms

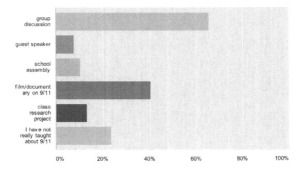

Q1 **What activities have you led to teach about 9/11? Please check the appropriate box and/or write in an activity you have implemented.**

Answered: 107   Skipped: 8

| Answer Choices | Responses | |
|---|---|---|
| group discussion | 65.42% | 70 |
| guest speaker | 7.48% | 8 |
| school assembly | 10.28% | 11 |
| film/documentary on 9/11 | 40.19% | 43 |
| class research project | 13.08% | 14 |
| I have not really taught about 9/11 | 23.36% | 25 |
| Total Respondents: 107 | | |

*Chart 1*

math and science. As I will relate in more detail in Chapter 4, one science teacher for example involved her students in a creative lesson regarding the engineering of the Trade Towers with regard to how the buildings would respond structurally to severe impact. Curriculum reformers and peace educators have long advocated this sort of integrated, interdisciplinary curriculum. The relevance or not of a particular topic is a matter of perception. One teacher commented, for example, that 9/11 is not within the curriculum as he teaches "the first half of American history", ending of course well before 2001. Do these constitute perceptual barriers, or barriers of professional culture which provides and rewards for the norm of adherence to the standardized curriculum, and punishes deviance from it?

I mentioned previously that there has been a proliferation of curriculum for teachers who do address 9/11. The New York Times, PBS, Teaching Tolerance and the Fordham Foundation have all developed lesson plans and units. Some of this curriculum is grounded in particular ideological views of 9/11. Teaching Tolerance (readers can visit them at teachingtolerance. org) is a project of the Southern Poverty Law Center; their organizational mission is to promote anti-bullying, peace and multicultural curriculum in classrooms nationally. Hence their curriculum provides for ways to combat

Inside the Classroom    49

Islamophobia, discusses bullying of Muslim students and similar. The Fordham Foundation exhibited quite a different focus, grounded in a concern for the perceived lack of patriotism in particularly civics and social studies curriculum today. In fact, their introduction seems to reveal that they believe there is a contradiction between a "patriotic" approach to teaching civics and American history, and taking a "multi-cultural approach". Given that the empirical demographics of the U.S. have always been multicultural, I do not see how such a contradiction can exist and am pretty obviously grounded in a different worldview. The point here is that teachers selecting either curriculum would in a sense be taking what some could perceive to be a political approach. Remember, teachers teaching 9/11 are doing so in the context of a highly partisan national culture, with education reform being one of the "proxy wars", if you will, of neoliberalism. We will revisit this more fully in the final chapters.

To return to the survey, are teachers using any of this curriculum? Largely, they are not. Only 32% of teachers who responded to my survey

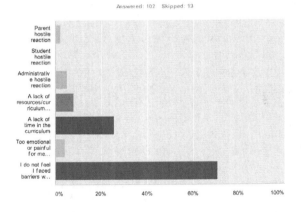

Chart 9

## 50  9/11 and Collective Memory in U.S. Classrooms

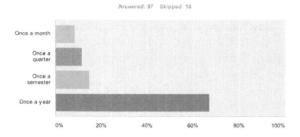

| Answer Choices | Responses | |
|---|---|---|
| Once a month | 8.25% | 8 |
| Once a quarter | 11.34% | 11 |
| Once a semester | 14.43% | 14 |
| Once a year | 67.01% | 65 |
| Total Respondents: 97 | | |

*Chart 4*

report using some sort of formal, published curriculum. Teachers specifically note using especially PBS, Teaching Tolerance, curriculum created by the Smithsonian, CNN, Brown University and the History Channel. PBS received the most mentions by teachers, followed by Teaching Tolerance. Clearly access to resources is not a significant barrier (unless one is in an especially marginalized school without internet access).

A main objective of this book is to begin painting a portrait overall of how (or indeed if) 9/11 is being taught in the classroom. Of the teachers who are addressing 9/11 at all, the majority (67%) only do so once a year (typically of course, this was on the commemoration date). This is why I report that 9/11, by and large, is not being taught in any substantive way.

Only 8% do so once a month, 11% once a quarter. When I asked for further comment here, responses ranged greatly. One teacher, for example, teaches a full three-week unit, while others report not addressing it at all or "here or there". Another teacher commented that s/he tries to use "teachable moments" to relate 9/11 to other subjects more formally in the curriculum. Interestingly, one survey participant shared that the students themselves will take the initiative and ask; this reinforces the responsibility we have as educators to facilitate discussion and understanding about 9/11. Education first and foremost should help us understand and act effectively in our world. Again, 9/11 was an event that bifurcated U.S. history and dramatically altered the landscape of the U.S. government particularly with regard to surveillance and security (Priest and Arkin 2011). Even current controversies such as the shockingly broad and global scale of NSA surveillance, revealed by whistleblower Edward Snowden, are related to this new landscape and the way in which we reshaped our national institutions and

Inside the Classroom 51

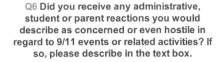

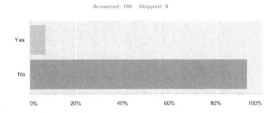

| Answer Choices | Responses |  |
|---|---|---|
| Yes | 6.60% | 7 |
| No | 93.40% | 99 |
| Total Respondents: 106 | | |

*Chart 6*

political culture in response to 9/11. Hence the high number of teachers finding it irrelevant to their curriculum was startling.

Very few teachers reported having experienced any sort of explicitly hostile reaction from a parent, student or administrator. 93%, an overwhelming number, said they did not feel they had experienced any hostile reactions from stakeholders.

Yet, while this occurred rarely, we should note that it did occur. Where teachers did experience such reactions, the details are revealing of the tensions and complexities of trying to address such a painful and controversial event whose impact America is absolutely still feeling. One teacher was actually fired from her job and went on to found her own charter school. Another teacher had students express that the images s/he presented were too upsetting, as the student(s) had a personal connection to the event. Another teacher was criticized for teaching about 9/11 as "it is not in the curriculum". A few teachers explicitly reported being told that teaching about 9/11 was just "too political". Some teachers received the concern that students were not alive at the time, or were still too young to be exposed (remember, the students in question are 6–12 graders). One teacher's reply seemed to despair of any response to 9/11 at her school at all: "No reaction positive or negative. It is not discussed or addressed at my school. There isn't even a moment of silence on 9/11." A final teacher (with a quick sense of humor), when asked if she had encountered any hostile reactions, replied "not yet".

Given the extremely painful and political nature of the topic, can we take this apparent "good news" at face value, or are there other factors we need to consider to properly understand this finding? I would argue that, like most other professionals, teachers have internalized the norms of how "far" they can go in expressing any political views they might hold. We

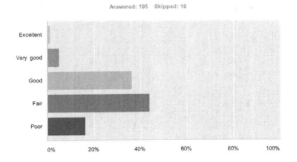

Chart 5

(I say we as I do not consider myself any exception to this generalization) have further internalized the professional value of neutrality. When such a value is consented to, it will not need to be explicitly enforced; the cultural norms of any group often only become visible when they are disregarded. As we will see the in the next chapter, the narrative which educators are presenting about 9/11 would most often not necessitate any such discipline. As a rule (though there are exceptions), this narrative is thin, rather surface and decontextualized, and thus might well not raise any alarm bells. If the narrative presented is not challenging any fundamental orthodoxy, there would be no need. This may explain the high percentage of teachers who self-report not having experienced any stakeholder hostile reactions.

Students, according to one teacher, expressed concern that such an attack as 9/11 could occur "and the responsible parties get away with it". Bin Laden was killed, of course, KSM is currently on trial and the hijackers themselves died. Military experts disagree on the extent to which Al Qaeda has been decimated, but the consensus is that they are not nearly as strong as they were before 9/11. So it is difficult to see how the attack was "gotten away with". This points to the worrisome gap of knowledge regarding the facts of 9/11, as many teachers noted. This problem will likely become worse as the years pass if parents, communities and schools do not address it. Indeed, only about 6% of teachers report that they consider their students' knowledge of the events of Sept. 11 either excellent or good.

*Inside the Classroom* 53

Several teachers I interviewed expressed concern about two particular challenges. One is the advent of the internet and the urgent need for students to learn how to distinguish between sources that are credible and sources that are not. While this type of critical thinking has always been a concern of educators, never has it been more pressing than now, the beginning of the digital information age. Misinformation and conspiracies regarding an event with the pain and impact of 9/11 are particularly toxic.

Many of my respondents also noted that with every passing year, of course, students recall less and less on their own what exactly did happen on 9/11. As one teacher noted, students understood 9/11, "in terms of planes crashing into buildings, not in as far as the details of the tragedy." In the next year or so, middle school students will be too young to recall 9/11 at all and will thus be entirely dependent on second-hand memories of parents, older relatives or friends, the media and of course, teachers. Historians consider events to be within "living memory" up to the third generation after a particular event, however, so 9/11 is still well within this range. According to my participants, students generally knew a basic sketch of the events (the U.S. was attacked by terrorists who crashed airliners into the Twin Towers) but understood far less of the details and historical context. "They understand", as one participant phrased it, "what happened but not the why." Another teacher echoed this observation almost exactly: "As each year passes, students know less about 9/11." Another concern (which I noticed myself during my years as an

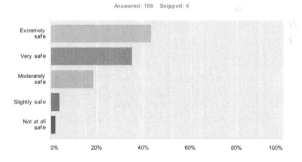

| Answer Choices | Responses | |
|---|---|---|
| Extremely safe | 43.12% | 47 |
| Very safe | 34.86% | 38 |
| Moderately safe | 18.35% | 20 |
| Slightly safe | 3.67% | 4 |
| Not at all safe | 1.83% | 2 |
| Total Respondents: 109 | | |

*Chart 8*

## 54  9/11 and Collective Memory in U.S. Classrooms

English teacher) is that some students came to the classroom with explicitly incorrect information, believing for example that we were attacked by Iraq. My participants with the richest curriculum on 9/11 explicitly intended to address this, as I will detail more in Chapter 4.

A central concern of critical peace educators, and many parents and teachers in general, has been how students are educated about dissent and whether or not we are equipping students with the skills and values needed to deepen democracy and further social justice. To better understand how teachers were experiencing this tension with respect to addressing what is surely the most controversial and difficult subject of U.S. history in decades, I asked my survey participants how academically free they felt at their school. On the surface, at least, the results were reassuring! 43% of teachers reported that they felt "extremely safe" and 35% reported that they felt "very safe".

The advantage of a mixed-methods study like this one is that it allows us to go behind these numbers. My qualitative interviews, as well as narrative (open-ended) comments from some teachers responding to the objective survey, strongly suggest teacher self-censorship. Several teachers elaborated on this sort of self-censorship in compelling ways. One participant, for example, noted that she took care to avoid "anti-Muslim sentiment" and "disturbing images". Expressing a view that is in my interpretation similar, a second respondent stressed the need for a multi-cultural, global approach to the teaching of 9/11. This teacher wrote: "As a teacher of all races, religions and the sort, we need to be very careful as to how we address the actions of this day and keep our personal feelings out of it. It needs to be taught to the younger sect on a 'global-scale' not a specific one." Several teachers suggested that the subject of 9/11 simply had not come up, suggesting the need for both teacher, administrative and even political leadership to ensure that 9/11 is in fact taught, and taught in a nuanced, global and complex manner.

My survey was designed to help us understand what teachers are doing in the classroom as regards teaching 9/11. To this end, I queried about this in the objective survey, as well as the interviews that I conducted. I asked teachers what sort of activities, if any, they actually implemented. As one might expect, leading group discussions was the most popular activity at 68%. A close second, with 40%, was showing students a documentary. Only 6% of teachers reported bringing in a guest speaker and 9% had their students attend a school assembly. About 10% of teachers responded that they engaged their students in an in-depth research project. And 23%, a number far too high in my view, responded that they have not addressed the subject of 9/11 at all.

Beyond the limited options I could offer in the format of a standardized survey, some teachers responded with notable details of addressing 9/11 in their classrooms in the open-ended part of the survey. One teacher has had students actually examine Al Qaeda manifestos. S/he then builds on this to teach students about contrasting, comparative political philosophies of all sorts, Eastern and Western, and even links this discussion to the current domestic debate regarding immigration. Most intriguing as it suggests a larger theme in this classroom of the social and historical dynamics of inclusion and exclusion. At the heart of politics is precisely this question. Polities—or imagined communities as Anderson would have it—are formed to empower, bind together and protect certain groups and thereby exclude and marginalize others. Nation-states explicitly enforce borders—boarders that have arguably been challenged as a result of economic and technological globalization. U.S. law defines citizenship, an act that inherently includes and excludes. Within Al Qaeda's ideology is a desire to restore the Caliphate, which would enforce a global divide between believers and infidels. Critical peace education, of course, would work to challenge all such divisions, empowering teachers and students to critically examine the historical details of how such dynamics of inclusion and exclusion emerged. Most urgently, critical peace education would facilitate understanding how such boundaries emerged and who such boundaries benefit. CPE can enable students to become engaged in building bridges across such barriers. This teacher appears to focus her curriculum on such questions.

Other reported classroom activities varied. One participant was involved in piloting new curriculum, while another was able to take students on a field trip to NYC! Another teacher used "primary source photos" to teach students about what occurred on 9/11; similarly a participant responded using editorials and news coverage from 9/11 and the immediate aftermath. (I did this myself with my high schoolers when I was teaching writing and literature, having saved a number of newspapers from Sept. 2001.) Other creative materials like children's literature or memoirs of survivors/witnesses were also used. The limitations of the anonymous online format prevented me from further follow up with these teachers (hence my decision to also conduct extended qualitative interviews) but the above offers a flavor of some of the activities occurring around 9/11 in today's classrooms.

## BARRIERS TO TEACHING ABOUT 9/11

This study was in part designed to help us, particularly critical peace educators, as well as social studies teachers and curriculum designers, begin understanding what teachers are doing in their classrooms around 9/11. I also, of course, wanted to help us as peace educators, curriculum designers, or just concerned teachers and parents, better grasp what sort of barriers teachers seemed to be facing as they taught about 9/11. As we can see in this graph, overwhelmingly, this barrier was time or curriculum!

Many teachers were quite explicit about this, and passionately eager to share their frustrations. As someone myself who taught middle and high school, I shared with them how readily I could relate. As a former English teacher, my curriculum was more flexible than most, and I still experienced

56   *9/11 and Collective Memory in U.S. Classrooms*

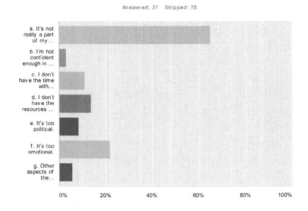

*Chart 2*

the frustrations of not being able to give my students as much flexibility as I had wanted to achieve a genuinely student-centered classroom. As one of my respondents wrote, "I'm sure if I looked . . . it would be relatively easy to find. However, we are under state testing parameters and curriculum, there isn't time for this topic to be taught in terms of getting children to understand and grasp the history and the tragedy." In the words of another teacher, "With day to day tasks, it doesn't cross my mind" (on her hand-written copy of this survey, she even draw a 'sad face' to presumably express her regret for not being able to find the time to teach something she must think important). My own current home state of Florida has been undergoing rapid, dramatic and highly controversial changes in preparation for the Common Core, but this reflects a national trend beyond Florida. 25% of teachers explicitly reported that they did not teach about Sept 11 because there was not enough time in the classroom to do so. Wrote another teacher, "With so much to cover, one day [to address 9/11] is really all that can be used." Another teacher commented on the objective survey, "I'm new here", suggesting that she felt unprepared to address such a subject and unable as a (tenuously employed) new teacher to step outside formalized standards. The barrier of time and the perception on the part of so many teachers that 9/11 is not a part of their curriculum is linked by the reality of centralized control of curriculum. This is why I argue that the barrier of time is not an organizational or curricular barrier; it is a *political* barrier. It represents priorities and constraints pertaining to what we think most important to teach and how we as a culture view and value (or fail to value) education.

Remember here that 65% of teachers who do not teach about 9/11 did not perceive 9/11 to be a part of their curriculum, a powerful number in my view. Possibly this is a perceptual barrier about what curriculum is and who determines that. Implicit in this view is, again, that curriculum is received and implemented by, not created by, classroom teachers. Notable also is the underlying assumption that curriculum is best divided into our current traditional academic disciplines, rather than integrated into an interdisciplinary approach and centered around compelling human challenges. Of course, critical peace educators would hope to empower teachers as public intellectuals, to use Henry Giroux's phrase, trusted to co-create essential curriculum with students and communities. Teachers, of course, are the ones who know their students best as learners. I would argue that this finding also reflects what I see as the most significant barrier to a complete and contextualized education about the 9/11 era—again, a lack of time. Implicit in the response that it is not a part of one's curriculum is the notion that curriculum ought to be divided by discipline (certainly an assumption that continues to organize the lives of students and teachers) and that other items need "covering".

The barrier teachers face of insufficient time to teach 9/11 speaks to the culture of standardization so prevalent in schools today. Curriculum is predetermined and centralized by the county or state, and time spent on something else is time away from one's formal obligations. The FCAT's (Florida's standardized achievement test) was singled out by one respondent as a reason for not teaching 9/11. My survey results suggest that several possible dynamics are present here within school culture. One possibility is that teachers have largely internalized that we as educators receive and teach curriculum, rather than creating it. This certainly does not apply to thousands of educators; it does not even apply uniformly to all of my participants, in either the survey or in-depth interviews. Yet the high percentage of teachers reporting that they do not address 9/11 at all, or only on the date itself, is revealing of where real power in U.S. schools lies. When it comes to creating and assessing curriculum, it does not lie with teachers. It lies with politicians and increasingly with wealthy neoliberal reformers who typically do not have any teaching expertise or experience (Ravitch 2013). Some teachers are able to creatively and resourcefully generate meaningful, relevant and interdisciplinary curriculum, finding ways to address the standards of a particular state test without "teaching to" it. Yet this is a monumental challenge, especially for new educators with

## 58  9/11 and Collective Memory in U.S. Classrooms

vanishing job security. Recall here that only twenty states mandate the teaching of 9/11; this may change in 2014 and thereafter depending on the adoption of the national Common Core (Hulette 2011). In an educational environment so perilous for teachers, with layoffs and high stakes testing exclusively used to determine a teacher's merit, it would be difficult indeed to color outside the proverbial lines. One teacher noted that 9/11 would be in his/her curriculum next year, but was not yet and so was not addressed. Another reported here that s/he was a new employee, suggesting a concern for her position, and so was unable to address 9/11. Feeling overwhelmed and needing more support was implied by another response to barriers to teaching about 9/11 in which the teacher reported s/he did not have a classroom. No doubt this was a barrier to his or her teaching in general.

Other challenges worth noting were certainly present for those who did report experiencing a barrier to teaching about 9/11, as one can see in the graphic above. 2% admitted to not feeling confident enough in their own knowledge of the events of 9/11. 9% responded that 9/11 is still simply too political to touch. One respondent noted that his conservative views could make teaching about 9/11 a challenge for him: "Potentially, as a political conservative, it would probably be difficult for me to be neutral with regards to our relative actions, which I have fully supported. You might say that I am quite 'hawk like'." As we'll see in the next chapter, teachers who viewed themselves as liberal or even peace activists expressed the same concern.

22%, a rather surprisingly high number in my view over a decade on, reported that teaching about 9/11 was still too emotionally painful to teach about. As this finding was from my survey, not the more in-depth interviews, I was not able to probe any further, but how interesting it would be to learn if these educators had some sort of personal connection to 9/11 or even experienced the death of a loved one. 14% of responding teachers felt they did not have the needed resources to teach about 9/11. 6% believed that other aspects of the curriculum were more important. A number of teachers responded that other teachers in their school addressed 9/11 (and so presumably they did not feel a need to). One commented that s/he discusses 9/11 before or after class but "never in the classroom" suggesting that this teacher is not comfortable doing so for whatever reason. I interpret this to suggest that this teacher does not feel 9/11 is a part of the formal classroom curriculum, but s/he is willing to discuss the events with interested students outside of the formal classroom space.

### DATA LIMITATIONS

Here I would like to be upfront regarding a few limitations of the data, so that the reader can judge and interpret as she would like. We did have to throw out a few surveys (from people not eligible such as guidance counselors or in a case of illegible handwriting). This impacted less than 1% of the surveys, leaving us with just over 150 valid responses. Self-selection also clearly seemed to be a factor; most of the teachers responding to the survey seemed to have something particular they wanted to say about teaching 9/11. Thus the number of teachers reporting that they address the topic in their classroom may well be somewhat inflated. Self-reporting is always a limitation in interview or survey-based studies. Other studies involving classroom observation would therefore be useful. We should also bear in mind that, as with any quantitative survey, the results represent a snapshot of what teachers have been thinking and doing as regards the teaching of 9/11. Replication will be important to further validate the results. Also, 9/11 occurred a mere twelve years ago—not long at all in historical terms. This is likely not enough time to truly come to terms with such a terribly transformative event. How can we tell students a coherent, complex and historical story of 9/11, and what it means, if we as adults have not yet done so? Beyond that it was an outrageous crime, and demands for increased security, I do not see that we have truly reflected as a nation.

Despite the above study limitations, such a national survey of how—or indeed *if*—teachers are bringing 9/11 into their classrooms, has not been undertaken prior to this study. Curriculum designers, teachers and administrators, community dialogue leaders, and peace and conflict professionals can use this data as we build our understanding of how the United States' chosen trauma is being taught and understood in our schools. Peace and conflict professionals, especially peace educators, must have this knowledge if we are to design processes which can attempt to interrupt the current escalating cycle of violence between the U.S. and allies, and "the Islamic World". Underlying the military and terrorist violence is, of course, structural and narrative violence. Teachers who work to provide students with a broad, historically contextualized and multi-vocal narrative contribute to narrative peace building, without which sustainable peace will not be possible. Next we will give such narrative space to teachers themselves, asking them to tell us in their own words and on their own terms how they have approached and experienced teaching about 9/11.

# 4 Educator Narratives of Teaching Terror

*"Where did everything go—how does one come to grips with the fact that one's loved ones are maybe now in this pile? There are no bones. There is dust."* Teacher 1

This chapter will describe the experiences of teachers, from a variety of disciplines (grades 6–12, again) working to address the events of 9/11 in their classrooms. My team and I conducted twenty-four in-depth, open-ended interviews, allowing teachers to tell us in their own words about their experiences of teaching such a painful and political topic in the context of scarce resources, hyper-standardization, high-stakes testing and ever more crowded and diverse classrooms. These interviews were either face to face or via the phone and typically lasted about 90 minutes. While the above chapter, based on the quantitative survey I conducted, gave us something of a snapshot of generally how often 9/11 is broached, what sort of activities teachers conduct and their impressions of what teaching about 9/11 is like, we need in-depth interviews to complete the picture of how this central event in U.S. history is being taught. Here teachers could go beyond the numbers to tell us directly what they are achieving, experiencing and facing in the classroom. I left the interviews largely open-ended but overall I asked teachers to tell me what sort of activities they had used, how they went about deciding what to do in the classroom, why they chose to ensure 9/11 was a part of their curriculum, how students, colleagues, parents and administrators had received their lessons, how they managed their own emotions while teaching about 9/11 and how they had navigated any relevant politics. I asked them to share any perceived problems or barriers to teaching about 9/11 and how they had handled them. For context I also asked them to tell me a bit about their school and classrooms—such as the resources available, school culture and demographics. Based on my interviews, some teachers are using teaching 9/11 to integrate and emphasize themes they already value. The themes that emerged the most clearly and frequently were tolerance, multiculturalism, diversity, critical thinking and patriotism.

Note any names that I use, or even gendered pronouns, are for disguise to keep the anonymity of the teachers who agreed to speak with me. Also in accordance with my agreement with participating teachers, I do not even refer to their school's location, though I do when relevant state the subject of the responding teacher. This cannot be enough to compromise anyone's anonymity. Underlining the politicization around 9/11 and I would argue the politicization of our schools in general, some of the teachers I spoke with confirmed their desire for this confidentiality.

## TEACHABLE MOMENTS: USING 9/11 TO ADDRESS SCHOOL AND COMMUNITY VIOLENCE

~*"How do you create change?"* Teacher 9 to her 12th graders

While none of the teachers I interviewed explicitly referred to themselves as a peace educator, about half of them did chronicle ways in which they employed a lesson about 9/11 to facilitate classroom dialogue about violence in general. Several teachers related the idea of teaching 9/11 to classroom-based efforts or formal lessons meant to reduce bullying and violence school wide. For example, Teacher 7 expressed that, during his unit on 9/11, he facilitates a discussion on the extent to which the class feels we in the U.S. are increasingly numb to the relentless violence around us. "Sometimes you get to immune to things" as a result of "media overload", he explained. He referred here not just to international violence like 9/11, but also to school shootings, domestic violence, violence in entertainment media, and everyday crime. Teacher 11 said her students asked about the recent (April 2013) bombing at the Boston Marathon during her facilitated discussion of 9/11 and they explored connections together.

Teacher intentions here seem to have been to cause students to question the use of violence as a means of resolving conflict and thus grapple with the consequences of violence on a variety of social levels. Teacher 3 shared two specific and disturbing examples. There is only a small percentage of Muslim students at her school and two Muslim middle school brothers in particular were bullied. Teacher 3 recalled seeing a bruise on one boy. When she reported it to her administration, no action was taken. This is a classic example of the "hidden curriculum" in that the lack of adult leadership here itself teaches that such bigoted violence is acceptable. In addition, a young Muslim, apparently very quiet, girl was also harassed some but, Teacher 3 reports, not like the boys were. Teacher 8 related a similar experience. At her previous school, a student from Pakistan ended up with a broken nose due to a bullying incident! She was not sure of how this situation was handled, and did not know of any similar experiences at her current school. It could be that there were no such incidents. Of course it could also be that she was not aware of them, or that the particular form of bullying that targets Muslims in particular is less present at this school due to its predominantly white demographics. Teacher 16 had a similar

## 62  9/11 and Collective Memory in U.S. Classrooms

observation of violence directed at Middle Eastern students. As she said, "I was told a lot of kids won't tell anyone they're Muslim . . . no one is going to complain because they're afraid to put a spotlight on this". She shared a specific incident, which she called racial profiling, of two Pakistani boys harassed her in schools' hallways as another student shouted, "You damn Middle Easterner". Other research on peace education and school violence shows the students themselves share the concern regarding the unwillingness or inability of responsible adults to address bullying (Duckworth, Williams and Allen 2012).

As a part of this theme of using lessons on 9/11 to teach about causes and impacts of violence more broadly, one teacher even said she considered the attacks of 9/11 to be a form of bullying in the sense of the use of violence to get what one wants. She was sharing with me how she has tried to convey the shock, pain and grief of 9/11 with students. I was intrigued by this suggestion of Al Qaeda as a bully. Strictly speaking the weaker party in a conflict would not be positioned this way but her meaning seemed clear. This particular educator shared with me that she had served in the military, as had her husband. An interview was the place to listen and to probe for more information, so I did not challenge her, but her metaphor of 9/11 as the U.S. being bullied suggests that structural power dynamics were not analyzed. It is obviously no defense of Al Qaeda's murder of innocent civilians to say this; the weaker party in a conflict can certainly resort to what most of us would consider to be acts of evil. The ability to "unpack", see and understand such structural power dynamics is, again, essential to a critical peace educator's classroom. Attacks by Al Qaeda on parties weaker than they, which they have committed frequently since 9/11, would be a better fit for a bullying frame. While this may seem like a trivial point, again, I believe it is essential to enable students to have the ability to analyze dynamics of power.

Teacher 9, a history, economics and government teacher, uses her week-long unit on 9/11 to involve students in conversations about school and community violence. She shared one especially harrowing story with me of her school being on lock down as the horror show of the massacre at Sandy Hook elementary unfolded in December 2012 (her school is only thirty minutes away). Teacher 9 took this nightmarish yet teachable moment, as well as her unit on 9/11, to challenge students to think about peer to peer conflict resolution and problem solving both in the classroom, school-wide and in the community. "Every student voice matters", she said, using the essential question of "what would you do?" (Essential questions in curriculum design are a "hook" question, a conceptual anchor for the lesson, which can fascinate students by making the concepts and skills relevant and relatable.) Such an approach invites students to integrate their classroom learning with what they observe in the school halls, at home and on their streets. My call has long been for such an approach, even then taking the next step to involve students in educational service to and partnership with adults in the community who are working on structural and other forms of violence in the local community.

This theme from my interviews, wherein teachers used a lesson on 9/11 to teach about violence more generally, reminds us of the wisdom of a classic approach of critical peace educators: the most powerful curriculum is interdisciplinary. Interdisciplinary curriculum is problem-based. In the case of 9/11 the problem facing all of us would be counterterrorism, liberty and security. Nearly any required school subject, as well as electives that are sometimes offered at the high school level (such as psychology) can be engaged in an integrated approach to teaching about 9/11. Naturally, history is involved, but so is literature. Think for example of the volumes of creative expression 9/11 generated as people grappled with it. As many teachers in my interviews are doing, 9/11 becomes in the classroom a compelling research, writing and presentation subject. One teacher presented his students with a class-wide research project focused specifically on constitutional issues. Another uses her position specifically as a world history teacher to explore with students the history of South East Asia, the Soviet Union and the Cold War.

What may be lacking to achieve an ideal multi-disciplinary approach to 9/11 (or most any other subject) is conscious coordination at the building or district level. While two of the 24 teachers I interviewed (both history and government teachers from different schools in different states) coordinated with one another via social media, there was nothing to suggest coordination with other teachers in their own schools or other teachers from different disciplines. Such coordination, of course, needs other teachers who are interested and willing to collaborate. In an environment where control over what occurs in the classroom is increasingly out of a teacher's hands, where pay is less and days are longer than they have been for teachers in decades, with vanishing job security, asking for the time and resources to undertake the sort of collaboration I am describing is daunting. Based on my own experience in the classroom when I advocated to have English and history courses at least partially co-taught, administrators are often reluctant to put the resources needed behind this important pedagogical technique because they are under pressure to prioritize budget cuts. Teachers would often need a planning period to design curriculum together, for example, and the sort of co-teaching involved in interdisciplinary curriculum means that several teachers may (at least for part of the day) be teaching in the same classroom together. In a neoliberal age of putting as many students together in the classroom with one teacher as the law will allow, an interdisciplinary approach likely seems unthinkable to too many administrators and school boards. Yet the compelling problems and timeless questions that humanity faces are inherently interdisciplinary! Until we commit to this shift in our national educational approach, too many students will not be empowered to see the connection between school subjects and their own lives. The teaching of 9/11 is no exception.

## 64   9/11 and Collective Memory in U.S. Classrooms

## MULTI-CULTURALISM, TOLERANCE
## AND DIVERSITY: "PEOPLE ARE PEOPLE"

In addition to using lessons on 9/11 to foster reflection and dialogue on school and community violence, teachers also reported using the teaching of 9/11 to address themes of multiculturalism and tolerance overall. Teacher 3 considered teaching "respect for one another" a key goal of her teaching. Teacher 2 related teaching about 9/11 to classroom lessons on racism. Further she relates 9/11 to some of the realities of her students' lives, some of whom had parents in jail or had been impacted by gun violence. Teacher 11 teaches world and American studies in a rural school with what she describes as predominantly white, male and conservative students. She expressed concern that her students were receiving prejudice against Muslims from home and felt a responsibility to do what she could from the classroom to counter this. She has often heard students state opinions "negative to all Muslims" and this precipitated her decision to begin her annual unit on religion with a lesson on tolerance. This involves asking students to define and discuss the concept. In what I take to be an effort to suggest that tolerance is bipartisan, she shares with students a quote from former President Bush, Jr. which relates how un-American bigotry is. Recalling one particular incident, a typically "great" student shocked her by announcing, "I hate all of them [Muslims]." She tells her students, "You can have an opinion, we need to make sure you're not attributing actions to an entire group". Like several other colleagues who also participated in this study, she points out to her students that "bad people can be a part of any group" and provides the example of Timothy McVeigh (who was behind the 1995 bombing of the Federal Building in OK). She further tries to break down stereotypes and hatred relating her lessons on Islam to some of the Muslims who are in her school (as a tiny minority, but there). Most of her Muslims students are from Eastern Europe, which usefully expands and complicates the images her students apparently have of their Muslim peers. When I asked her how effective she felt this lesson was, she reflected that "usually they [the students] apologize" for anything they realize they should not have said. She did express concern about the impact of these lessons on tolerance, however, and indeed, the outcome of such peace education is very difficult to measure. "I was afraid things would go off the rails", she said, when she planned a lesson in which students would read and respond to an opinion article on what anti-Muslim activists successfully branded the "Ground Zero Mosque". Perhaps (or perhaps not) because she had to leave the class with a sub that day, "even though we talked about tolerance, when it came to that mosque, they weren't very tolerant". During this story, Teacher 11 suggested that the virulence of some student responses gave her pause to attempt deeper, more political discussions related to 9/11, causing her to avoid them. In her own words: "I was a little worried after reading some of their responses" to the op-ed on the Islamic Community Center in Manhattan (tarred as the "Ground Zero Mosque"). This reflects, in my analysis, the reality that building a true school (and community) culture of peace is a year-long challenge. We cannot simply look to a few lessons or a few specific teachers to counter deeply entrenched historical and cultural trends. Nor should we ask teachers to address such traumatic and politically charged subjects without training and support. While plenty of teacher education programs offer theory and discussion on ethnicity, culture and other diversities in the classroom, teachers receive far less *practice* in inter-cultural facilitation. Experience and time are necessary for teachers, for whom group facilitation is a key skill, to develop the needed skill and confidence.

Teacher 1 uses her science curriculum to facilitate a discussion about 9/11 in general and a lesson on the need for tolerance and the value of diversities. Her school has, she noted, a Pakistani and an Indian student, who she reports worked together in her classroom. It is also home to a number of Jewish and Muslim students. This teacher, who not incidentally is at a public charter school, is responsible for state testing and standards but appeared to have more control than the average public school teacher over how to go about meeting those standards. Her school geographically is close enough to Washington DC that her own memories of Sept 11 are still powerful for her. She is also a seasoned teacher, with the experience and confidence necessary to address painful, divisive and complex topics.

Teacher 3 was committed to teaching values and skills of multiculturalism and tolerance beyond 9/11. She shared that she thinks her students have been very responsive to her on themes of peace and unity as she is a former soldier and as such has lived in Germany and Japan and thus is able to speak about other cultures from a first hand perspective. One wonders how many teachers have this background or ability. Yet even she found developing themes of multiculturalism school-wide exceedingly difficult. Her challenges reflected budget austerity in her state's schools and legal bureaucracy. Her efforts to excite kids about other cultures through foods from around the world were canceled by her administration in fear of law suits which might emerge if the food was not safe. While her efforts to host a "Mix It Up" day at school (see http://www.tolerance.org/mix-it-up/what-is-mix) were not prohibited by administration, implementing proved impossible as the administration would not staff it and no other teachers at this school volunteered. During a Mix It Up day, students are encouraged to have lunch and other activities with students they typically do not spend time with, ideally students of other backgrounds. District-wide and school-wide resources and leadership are clearly necessary for even such simple efforts to foster a culture of peace in a school to succeed.

Teacher 6 (in a public charter school which she founded) related 9/11 to other forms of injustice and, though she didn't use the term, essentially used it to teach about structural violence and causes of violence in general. For example, she taught about unequal uses of energy resources globally,

## 66 *9/11 and Collective Memory in U.S. Classrooms*

causes of rape and the culture of misogyny, and exploitation of migrant labor. Not coincidentally, this was the teacher who was fired for insubordination. Refusing to let this intimidate her, she went on to found her own school. This educator exemplified teaching of a curriculum centered around themes of peace and justice; her approach to teaching 9/11 was an extension of this thematic anchor. One morning, for example, she took students to a street corner where migrant laborers were known to be and invited students to talk with them as a field-trip supplement to their readings and debates on unemployment, immigration, racism and labor. This is true experiential learning—and also, this educator suspects, the lesson that got her fired. Apparently her use with the students of the word "solidarity" was especially problematic for her administrators.

Her approach to teaching 9/11 is similarly focused on student engagement and social justice. She was one of the minority of teachers who grounds her unit on 9/11 in deep historical context. Her approach is overtly critical of the United States, which some may applaud and some may find unprofessional and inappropriate. For my part, it is consistent with critical peace education to question violence (state violence included), scrutinize institutional power and encourage students to do the same. If schools are to be more than instruments of the state, teachers and students must be free to criticize policy when they think it necessary. In the tradition of and as a student of educational philosophers such as John Dewey, Maria Montessori and Paolo Freire, I argue that such is critical to the health and indeed survival of any democracy.

Teacher 6 also centered much of her curriculum around themes of nonviolence, multi-culturalism and social justice. Her teaching of 9/11 was no exception. From the standpoint of valuing social justice and diversity, as well as valuing critical thinking as an educational objective, she was concerned that "they [her students] have no idea why they think Muslims hate America". So a comprehensive and responsible curriculum, from her view, would teach kids to break this down and analyze where such views may have come from. How did the stereotypes from TV and other media compare to the facts? Who would put such misinformation out into the public sphere and why?

9/11, to again state the obvious, is unavoidably political and controversial. There was a wide range of the how deeply, if you will, teachers waded into the controversy. Teachers responding to my interviews in general used activities like documentaries and group discussion to try to correct misinformation that students might have had (like Iraq being involved in 9/11) or obvious bigotry against Muslims. A couple of teachers reported to me being rather shocked at student descriptions of Muslims as violent or as terrorists. One teacher I interviewed specifically mentioned her discomfort with her students' apparently enthusiastic support for torture. Some teachers, especially the history and English teachers among the group I interviewed, used the teaching of 9/11 to engage debate to the extent possible about issues like

*Educator Narratives of Teaching Terror*   67

torture, Gitmo, Iraq, and other controversies that have arisen as a result of the U.S. national response to 9/11.

Several of these teachers, however, noted that engaging these debates has been difficult for a couple of reasons. Some of these challenges relate to the neoliberal context of budget cuts, widespread disregard for teachers and centralized control of curriculum. In the words of Teacher 7, most years when teaching about 9/11 he did not "go into full-blown lessons mainly because of time." Others barriers are more methodological. For one, 9/11, falling in the calendar year as it does, tends to be right near the beginning of school. This leaves not much time to establish beginning of year classroom routines and procedures, build up the community of trust and provide students with the needed background to really have a proper debate about these kinds of issues. Much background on U.S. foreign policy, U.S. government and history, current events, as well as much history of the Middle East, is required. Given that the typical school system begins early Sept, there is simply not enough time for a meaningful unit. Odd as it may seem, teaching about 9/11 is best separated from a commemoration of the date itself for this reason (year-round schools might not face this challenge).

Another challenge facing teachers teaching about 9/11 (which must also apply to the teaching of other difficult historical events) is the necessary level of expertise—or at least one's confidence in one's expertise. One government teacher shared with me that he would need to study to feel assured teaching a lesson on Islam in the Middle East, for example. There is also the complexity, even the pedagogical danger, of teaching about Islam on a unit or lesson on 9/11. The teachers I spoke with expressed deep concern about accuracy, nuance of presentation and presenting the facts of the events of 9/11 without reproducing Islamophobia, intolerance or stereotypes in the classroom. Some teachers (with the protection of confidentiality and anonymity no doubt) expressed concern about the ability of some of their colleagues to adequately present the complete context and history of 9/11. One teacher I spoke with stated that she would not really want teachers teaching about 9/11 without a set curriculum to guide them; her concerns were both breath and depth of the necessary knowledge, as well as the professionalism and skill set to remain (in her words) unbiased regarding such emotional material.

While a lack of access to quality curriculum did not emerge in my survey data as a significant barrier to teaching about 9/11, in the in-depth interviews some teachers did express concern about the depth of presentation of 9/11 in the history books and found themselves having to supplement quite a bit. One teacher (a middle school reading teacher) expressed concern about a lack of themes of tolerance and multi-culturalism in the textbooks. She believes it is "important for children to know about other cultures and countries" and expressed that "my whole message is peace and unity". Accordingly she had to take extra time to supplement the standardized curriculum.

## 68    *9/11 and Collective Memory in U.S. Classrooms*

Teacher 8 has had students journal each year (recall she's an English teacher) since 9/11 and then has the kids of the present year read student journals from years past. She wants students to hear directly from their peers what their memories of that day were. This began, she said, on 9/11 itself. Her students of course were afraid and distracted (a luxury teachers that day did not have, or at least they could not allow it to show) and so she adapted on the spot. She was teaching juniors at the time and let them simply free-write about whatever they were thinking and feeling at the time instead of the planned lesson. Each subsequent year, she has had her students free-write about their memories of 9/11, though this has become more and more difficult for the student with each passing year as distance from 2001 increases. To foster student understanding of what it was like to experience that day, she has recently begun keeping (with student permission) some of the free-writes from years past to collect in a binder. She shares this with present students before asking them to write about their own understanding or memories of 9/11. Next year, Teacher 8 said, she plans to have students type up the previous year's free-writes to see "what former students had to say". From a narrative peace building perspective, what's striking about this is the instinct on her part to foster a sense of collective memory and to bring students as close as she reasonably could from her classroom (geographically not near PA, NYC or Washington, DC) to understanding the direct, visceral experience of Sept 11.

Narrative peace building will be a focus of the final chapter. For now, we can see Teacher 8's efforts, like those of her colleagues, to try to prevent the internalization of a collective narrative of Islam being a violent religion or of Muslims/Arabs (too often conflated as the same thing) being terrorists. For example, Teacher 8 has engaged local Muslim guest speakers to interrupt and counter images students arrived in her classroom with of Muslims as evil, anti-American and so forth. It is critical to understand that, especially in the post-9/11 era, our students arrive with this narrative as a "default". Narrative peace building theory demonstrates that without actively engaging to disrupt and replace such narratives, their inertia will continue. This will in turn continue to feed the already self-sustaining conflict between the U.S. and the "Muslim World". Teacher 8 made a somewhat similar observation: she shared that, especially as the years have slipped away since 2001, she increasingly will "have to clarify" what really happened on 9/11 (that Iraq, for example, was not responsible for the attacks, a classic and troubling misconception of the post-9/11 generation). She taught them about the definition of stereotypes and "corrected", in her words, the students when they expressed a stereotype. This occurred particularly when students would express hatred for Muslims in their free-writes. She pointed out here that there is only a tiny percentage of Muslims at her school. When I probed to ask how the students responded to the correction, she explained, "I'm an authority figure, I rarely have the kids argue with me". Yet I wondered still, as she herself may wonder, if the students internalized her guidance against stereotyping or if they simply accommodated her authority. As Teacher 8 herself reflected, "I'm not sure if that gets through to them". Still, she expressed faith that "there is a knee jerk reaction and then what they rationally believe". The highest purpose of education is exactly to move us beyond our "knee-jerk reactions". Research is needed here to understand more clearly not just how teachers are teaching 9/11, but what in fact students are learning. Their views may well change as they continue to mature and as their life experience deepens and broadens—or not.

As a part of destabilizing the narrative that Muslims are violent extremists (itself an extremist narrative), Teacher 8 discusses terrorism and extremism as a whole, rather than solely examining Islamic extremism. She gives students examples of Christian extremists who have targeted doctors and clinics providing abortions to counter the simplistic narrative of a one-to-one equivalence of Islam to terrorism. "They think it's [Islam's] a pretty violent culture", she said, so these efforts to disrupt and replace that narrative are urgent from a peace building, or even conflict prevention, perspective. While a minority of their colleagues, the teachers who use their classrooms to foster dialogues about the causes of violence, stereotypes, racism and inequalities make a real contribution to building a culture of peace.

Along those lines, Teacher 10 (a teacher of high school history who has been teaching for eight years) used a documentary entitled, "Fordson: Faith, Football and Fasting", which focuses on Muslim Americans in Dearborn, MI, known for the large Arab American diaspora there. It explores the Muslim perspective on how 9/11 changed the United States. The documentary includes a young Muslim boy being arrested. As Teacher 10 observed, "9/11 turned everything into a stereotype" and so showing the documentary "is very eye-opening" for the students. This school, Teacher 10 reported, is about 80% white, 10% Hispanic and 10% other, so this activity seems to add a necessary perspective for the students who would not likely encounter it otherwise.

A focus on peace, nonviolence and tolerance also anchored Teacher 9's curriculum on 9/11. Most Americans view 9/11 as an era, not just a day; this seems to be part of the collective narrative forming in our national psyche. Accordingly, as I have been chronicling, teachers who feel they have the luxury (or take the luxury) of time to spend more than one 45 minute class period on 9/11 teach about how the U.S. and other countries responded to 9/11. During one such classroom dialogue, many of Teacher 9's students were expressing concern about what anti-Muslim activists termed (and the media parroted) the "9/11 Mosque" or sometimes the "Ground Zero Mosque". This, the reader will probably recall, was an Islamic Cultural Center planned about six or so blocks away from Ground Zero. To challenge and engage her students' concerns, Teacher 9 used the dialogue to teach in more depth about the Bill of Rights, focusing as one would imagine in particular on the freedom of religion and the freedom of assembly.

70 *9/11 and Collective Memory in U.S. Classrooms*

Teacher 19, like some of his colleagues, is proactive and intentional in working to bring themes of peace and diversity into his classroom. A veteran of the classroom, he has taught for over thirty years and currently teaches 7th-grade social studies. He shared that his Quaker beliefs were foundational to his approach. His school has become progressively more diverse over the past several years, which he feels has made it ever more necessary to implement explicit peace education to teach increasingly multicultural students (and parents!) to better understand the other cultures in the schools with them. He shared a disturbing situation that may in fact be rather common based on how frequently it has come up anecdotally in my research (my research design did not focus on this so I can't really make an empirical claim based on my data regarding the following). What he describes as an activist group of Christian parents have vocally resisted his attempts to maintain a rich ten-week unit that he teaches on world religions. This of course includes Islam, Judaism, Christianity, Hinduism, and Buddhism, among others. It seems one of the parents in particular, in what he seemed to view as an extreme, commented that he took too long to teach about the Holocaust. This Christian activist parent then, Teacher 19 shared, went on to wonder aloud if "the Jews" had lobbied or pushed him into it. At this narrative, I suggested that he was in some important ways teaching the parents as well. He laughed and said he hoped so. This has become especially important to him given that it seems some of the Arab and/or Muslim students and families in the school community have expressed feeling "ostracized" due to the vocal advocacy of this activist Christian parent group. In his words, "we've had a couple of instances of adults behaving badly". It seems the Holocaust unit has elicited the most push-back (no doubt if he entertained a whole unit on 9/11 this would receive push-back as well). One parent from this group asserted his view that Teacher 19 was not "allowed" to teach a religion. He replied that he is not teaching a religion, he is teaching *about* religion and referred the group to the state's standards. He suggested that if their concerns continued, they were welcome to visit his classroom and speak with the Superintendent.

He has no illusions, though, that a non-tenured teacher, or a teacher with tenure but perhaps less longevity, would have had a more difficult time with this situation. As he explained, "As a non-tenured teacher it's difficult." It is not possible to adequately educate students about what I call the "9/11 era" without addressing the role of Islam, divergent views of Islam and the rise of Islamophobia. Yet the current seemingly "perfect storm" of centralized state standards, high-stakes scantron testing and heightened partisanship and politicization over the very place and existence of a multicultural approach in our classrooms is not lost on newer teachers. This is a chilling climate in which to engage contested, traumatic history.

Teacher 19 crafted his curriculum on 9/11 to foster a sense of commonalities and unity among his students. In what seems to prevail as the most popular 9/11 lesson among the teachers I interviewed, he asks his students

## Educator Narratives of Teaching Terror   71

to conduct an interview at home with an older brother or sister, or a parent. Like his colleagues, he of course has taken note of how students each year on from 9/11 knew and felt less and less about this transformational chosen trauma. He shaped the discussion when they share about their interviews to ensure students understand that their classmates from all various ethnic backgrounds—including Muslim and/or Arab—had been impacted by 9/11. As he put it, "it's always a win when you can get the kids and adults to see commonalities" among one another.

Another narrative he shared is illustrative of how he anchors his curriculum around the themes of peace and justice, both with respect to his 9/11 lessons, the connections he makes with that to his ten-week unit on comparative religions, and his curriculum in general. A key insight for effective critical peace education lies herein: themes of peace and justice are not tangential. They must be explicit and consistent throughout the year. For the most impact, such curriculum must be a part of a larger effort to foster a culture of peace throughout the whole school, ideally in partnership with the larger community. We will return to this in the final chapter. At this point, a narrative this teacher shared with me is illustrative. His in depth unit on comparative religion, the one he feels is now so threatened by centralized state standards, becomes an opportunity for marginalized students to find their voice and share who they are with the rest of the class. "This is your chance to shine", he tells them, inviting them to supplement or correct him if he inadvertently provides what they view as poor information on their faith. One young girl from Bosnia in his class recently asked, during a lesson on the Holocaust, if she could share her own family's experience of political violence and ultimately the genocide in Srebrenica (in eastern Bosnia) in 1995. Of course he welcomed her request. It seems her parents met in a refugee camp as a result of being displaced by the war. She shared their experiences and spoke about her family's direct experience with genocide. This "made my year", Teacher 19 reported. Not only do such moments engage students in the learning of history, they develop both curiosity and empathy, key outcomes of peace education. In this manner themes of multiculturalism and tolerance, and the understanding of the horrific political violence that results when those are absent from a community, were central to this classroom.

The teaching of 9/11 for him was no exception. On the day of 9/11 itself, Teacher 19 shares with students his memories, expressing a desire to convey to them the fear and pain and sheer emotion of that day. Like some of the other teachers I interviewed, he is not too far a drive from Ground Zero. He shares the sights, sounds and memories of the day with his students. He also uses a children's book *14 Cows for America*. Readers may recall the story of the Maasi tribe in Kenya who learned of 9/11 months after the fact. Upon hearing of the news of the mass murder from a Kenyan medical student who had been studying in the U.S. on 9/11, and applying the tribe's principles of "Ubuntu" (a belief in human solidarity that says 'I

## 72  9/11 and Collective Memory in U.S. Classrooms

am because you are'), the tribe offered fourteen cows as a gift of honor to U.S. diplomats. Cows are sacred in this culture and represent great wealth. As the books reads, "Because there is no nation so mighty that it cannot be wounded, nor people so small they cannot offer mighty comfort." Teacher 19 describes this lesson as his "go to" on teaching the subject of 9/11. Given that 9/11 falls so close to the beginning of the year, he also uses this lesson to introduce the idea of culture in general to students. As for the students, "they get it . . . they really get it on a level they understand." He noted that this is the power of storytelling, which has always been a universal human means of communication, teaching and learning. Succinctly, "it sticks", he says. This is fortunate as he confirms that he, like so many of his colleagues, struggles to find time to teach 9/11 as fully as he would like.

Teacher 12 shared with me a tension between the desire to teach curriculum which she knows will meet students' social and emotional needs (that is, curriculum themed around peace, justice, diversity) and the presumed, internalized professional standard of being "unbiased". Desiring to focus on these themes, she admired the NJ-based curriculum "Learning from the Challenges of Our Time" (which may well soon be phased out due to Common Core) despite being in another state. She praises it for its focus on the concept of the creation of historical memory, and its relevance to South Africa and Rwanda, among others. It further includes notions of service, reconciliation and "building a better future". She lamented that she cannot really use it and enthused that she would "be all over it" if she had the luxury of time. Given the constraints of her standardized curriculum, she does her best to weave these themes throughout her curriculum as she can. She especially weaves in themes of people being caught in a "cycle of violence and revenge". She noted that it was difficult to find curriculum that she considered to be appropriate (written at an appropriate reading level) and that it was particularly hard to find curriculum on the "lead up" to 9/11, as she put it. She emphasizes the need to respect different backgrounds, which of course will often lead to differing opinions on events. A central goal for her was to develop a classroom culture of peace by emphasizing hope, humanity and heroism in even the worst events of history. In her words, she wants to show students, "we have a choice to focus on the horribleness or the heroism and courage of people caught up in" violent events like 9/11. Desiring to emphasize the destructive nature of hate and the need for tolerance, she relates the conflict involving FL Pastor Terry Jones (of "Burn a Quran Day" infamy) to her lesson on 9/11. In addition, she spends a full week discussing the concept and workings of stereotypes with her students. Regarding the teaching of 9/11 specifically, she finds like her colleagues do that "kids come in thinking all Muslims are terrorists". Given her learning goals of peace and justice, she notes, "I go after that really hard" and laughs that she "basically program[s] them". She also invites local Christian, Jewish and Muslim parents into her classroom to answer student questions about the tenants of their faiths. Her unit on the monotheistic religions has not been entirely without controversy; she jokes with me that she calls it "Angry Parent Week". Still, she says, it gives her students a "realistic" view of these religions. She expresses certainty that her efforts here are a success: "the majority of them get it!" and "can easily see" how stereotypes form and how destructive they can be. One reason for this, she suggests, is that she provides an example bound to resonate with every student in her class: stereotypes of teenagers! Teacher 12 reports that her students "turn out to be logical, reasonable and compassionate" people (counter to many youth stereotypes). She emphasized, "I am repeatedly, consistently impressed with the ability of my students to respectfully disagree with each other". Here she is bringing into her classroom, at least based on these activities, both a culture of peace as well as the development of the skills essential for effective, critical citizenship in a democracy. She is intentional about wanting to send them off into the world at the school year's end with a message of peace, telling them that their civility and respect towards one another "gives [her] hope in a dark world". No one can say if this flame she tries to light is indeed lit except the students themselves but her classroom, and in particular her lessons on terrorism and 9/11, are centered around themes of building peace.

Teacher 16 was similarly proactive and explicit in her approach to weaving themes of diversity, peace and multi-culturalism into her classroom. Teaching about 9/11 is mandated in her state (unlike most states) and she invites her English students to write about a time they felt discriminated against. She chooses this approach because for her, "discrimination is the first thing that comes to my mind when I think of 9/11—in other classes they will get the party line". She aims to interrupt and complicate the narrative of Muslims as violent extremists. One lesson involves a documentary named *A Land Called Paradise*. A man interviewed in the video says, "My religion was hijacked", a humanizing moment which she uses as an opening into discussion of the Middle East and Islam. She then links this to the kinds of diversity in her own classroom, asking students to create a class video reflecting on one thing they would want people to know about them that people often get wrong. Some of her Hispanic students especially were engaged in this activity, sharing observations such as "I'm legal" (contrary to common perceptions), or "I'm Latina *and* I'm Muslim". This is particularly empowering and useful for building a school culture of peace given that she observed some of her Muslim students do not identify themselves as such for fear of being ostracized or even attacked.

Illustrating the links between critical thinking and peace education, Teacher 16 also worked to challenge her students ("38 reluctant freshman", as she memorably described them) to consider simplistic, Manichean worldviews and to do the difficult emotional and intellectual work of considering the consequences of becoming entrapped in a cycle of revenge. Before returning to the high school classroom, she was involved in researching the Holocaust as a Holocaust Museum Fellow and reflected: "As a Holocaust

74 *9/11 and Collective Memory in U.S. Classrooms*

researcher, I find it dangerous to dwell so much on your victimhood and feel entitled to do whatever . . . for me [teaching] 9/11 is complicated. Think of Pearl Harbor and what came of that? Internment. We have to be more effective and critical in how we think and teach about it and not just wallow in it". She further worked to incorporate a diversity of perspectives on 9/11 into her lessons and classroom discussion. "When we talk about 9/11", she said, "you have to look at a multiplicity of voices—not just American voices—what was the world thinking?" I have found myself doing the same with my graduate students, making sure to remind them for example that over 80 countries lost people on 9/11, not just the U.S., an effort to challenge overly simplistic understandings.

Teacher 23 provided a further example of especially English and social studies teachers viewing their lessons or units on 9/11 as a means of raising themes of tolerance, diversity and peace. She teaches in a rural Midwestern school without much racial, ethnic or religious diversity. 9/11 falls near the beginning of the school year, which for many high school English teachers means teaching Arthur Miller's *The Crucible*. As those who have enjoyed this play will know, a central theme of it is the dangerous result of fear and how contagious paranoia can be when security fears are played upon. Readers may remember that Miller's play was an allegory for the McCarthy era and his "witch hunts" for Communists within the U.S. government; to help students make this connection she shows them *Good Night and Good Luck*. Teacher 23 asks students to consider parallels between these areas in U.S. history and current treatment and views of American Muslims, noting that Pres. George W. Bush called upon Americans to not stereotype or target Muslims in the aftermath of the attacks. As she said, "We focus on how we can control mass hysteria. . . . We talk about empathy and in the panic forgetting to control mass hysteria". She teaches the concept of scapegoating and marginalization and ultimately asks students to write about if they believe that mass panic in societies can in fact be controlled.

The teacher narratives above demonstrate specific lessons and approaches that center 9/11 curriculum around essential concepts such as diversity, tolerance and multiculturalism. Especially striking is how difficult recent curriculum battles regarding standardization, high stakes testing and even tenure have made the inclusion of such curriculum. For some who perceive multicultural or peace-centered curriculum to be at odds with patriotism, this is of course one of the goals. To the complex theme of patriotism we now turn.

## TEACHING 9/11 AS ACT OF PATRIOTIC DUTY: "THE KIDS NEED TO NEVER FORGET"

9/11, on your calendar, will likely be called "Patriot's Day". Many Americans consider the simple act of memorial to be an act of patriotism. In fact,

## Educator Narratives of Teaching Terror    75

most of us likely cannot imagine allowing the day to pass without some sort of remembrance. This means it is worth considering in what specific ways we remember 9/11, and whether these particularities are likely to create healing and strength, or further trauma, division, and violent conflict. What we mean by patriotism must also urgently be considered. How do we engage students not just in dialogues about the nature of democracy, but actively engage students in school-based and community democratic processes? How do we as educators define this personal and complicated word? As we will see below, nearly each teacher I spoke with viewed teaching about 9/11 as a patriotic duty (whether it was in the state standardized curriculum or not). What was less clear and uniform from teacher to teacher is how that person understood patriotism and what they meant by patriotism. A variety of views on this is appropriate and to be expected in a free society. Many of the teachers I spoke with seem to define at least their patriotism as

1. Preserving the memories and honoring the victims of 9/11.
2. Impressing upon students the import, intensity and immediacy of the events of 9/11 from an emotional and experiential, not just an intellectual, perspective.
3. Ensuring students understand, and think deeply and critically about, the nature of the U.S. response to 9/11 and the immense ways in which it changed us.

Twenty-two out of the twenty-four teachers I sat down with specifically mentioned feeling obligated as an American to ensure that the victims and all impacted directly by 9/11 are not forgotten. For Teacher 21, 9/11 is something students need to not just know about, but care about and understand. He said, "It's something kids need to understand and never forget. We have to teach them what happened and how it affected us." His goal for students was this appreciation, rather than historical details or ensuing political debates. In his words, "Sometimes, well, we'll talk about how it affected people of the Islamic faith, but not a lot because it's mostly about how we healed." The grief, the facts and emotions and subsequent healing were the most salient topics for his 8th-grade social studies students. To achieve this, he uses a more structured version of a common approach of teachers addressing 9/11, which is to ask students to gather oral histories at home. He asks his students to interview three people who must be of three different age groups, a creative means of diversifying perspectives. He provides interview questions for the students, at least one of which explicitly focuses on emotion. Students next must find similarities and differences that emerge from their interviews. He then asks students to present their findings. In addition, it turns out that a substitute teacher at his school lost her brother; she has sometimes discussed her experiences for the school. He has consistently found positive experiences, with no concerns from parents

## 76  9/11 and Collective Memory in U.S. Classrooms

or others. Parents, he reports, have expressed appreciation for his lessons, valuing the opportunity to be involved with their child's education.

Teacher 15 stated simply, "I just feel personal responsibility" to teach 9/11. Teacher 10 said that his school does a building-wide moment of silence. On September 11, 2002, his students hand-made an American flag. This project, he felt, led to "an awakening" with respect to the terrible gravity and import of 9/11. Teacher 10 also faced the barrier some of his colleagues faced, namely the lack of formal, state curriculum regarding 9/11. This is why he broached 9/11 only on the anniversary date. It was not a part of the history or social science curriculum but, he said, "I made it part of it". He continued, "a good teacher is going to get the job done". Patriotism was clearly a key motivator for this teacher working to bring 9/11 into the classroom. I raised the question of how these teachers define and understand patriotism; Teacher 10 seems to understand it to involve national unity. It relates to "the whole idea of coming together as a country. . . . we hadn't had to come together as a country like that in a long time". He went on to express regret that such unity has not lasted. He was concerned specifically about the tiny percentage of Americans directly impacted by the wars which 9/11 spawned—the invasions of Iraq and Afghanistan. He was also concerned about the remaining divide between the North and South. In this sense, it was his view that 9/11 changed America for better and for worse; he felt our divisions regarding how to best respond to terrorism reflected cultural and ideological battles from the past.

Some teachers I spoke with seemed to understand patriotism, in the context of teaching about 9/11 at least, as having a clear, accurate and sufficiently profound understanding of the pain it caused and how dramatically it changed America as a nation. Teacher 5, a 7th-grade civics teacher, worried that his students "felt indifferent . . . they could not relate and seemed to care less about the topic". His pedagogical goal, then, was to counter this perceived apathy. His personal connection to 9/11 was bound up with his notion of patriotism and the teaching of 9/11 as his uncle, a Colonel in the Army, was working at the Pentagon on 9/11. To engage his diverse classroom, he asked students to read various news articles which had covered the events of 9/11. He also designed a "home learning experience" which asks students to dialogue with their parents. He also asked them to view specific videos from 9/11 to "make a personal connection" to the events of that day. Again we note the understanding of patriotism, with respect to teaching and learning about 9/11, entails a direct, emotional and intimate understanding not just of what happened on 9/11, but how it felt. Imparting the impact of the experience here seems to be the objective—yet without causing students trauma or without reproducing Islamophobic stereotypes. The desire seems to be for an almost phenomenological understanding of the attacks, with the underlying belief that one's education about American history and as an American citizen is not complete otherwise. As I was suggesting in Chapter Two, this implies that not just understanding but

*Educator Narratives of Teaching Terror* 77

*relating to and identifying with* the events of 9/11 is now seen as a necessary aspect of American patriotism. This kind of reshaping of national identity is a key signifier of the presence of a chosen trauma.

Teacher 5 also worked to counter perceived student apathy by facilitating discussions on the difficult issues that have faced us since 9/11. He specifically cited how governments have responded to other acts of terrorism, the perennial tension between public safety and individual liberty, and "why the government under the Bush administration expanded to create the Dept. of Homeland Security". He shared that he found his students (at what some might see as too young an age) were informed and able to discuss such topics. The demographics of this teacher's urban school might have caused another teacher to shy away, with 79% of his students receiving free or reduced lunch under Title I. He reports that on his state's standardized tests, his students receive a whole range of scores, from the highest of 3–5 to the lowest of 1's and 2's. For the record, his school has 50% Hispanic students, 38% African American, 12% white and 2% Asian.

Teacher 20's activities focused on the heroism of first responders on 9/11. He shared "Last Man Down" with his 7th-grade World History students, the story of a firefighter who was trapped in one of the Twin Towers and survived. He then contrasts this narrative with one that he apparently took from an NPR broadcast of a victim of 9/11 who did not survive the attacks but died shortly after being able to call his wife. He seems, like other educators teaching 9/11, to value and have as an objective the affective experience: "You know after that there are no dry eyes in the classroom." He enjoys teaching about 9/11 due, of course, to its terrible importance to U.S. and world history. To aid in getting himself into the right emotional frame of mind, he reports that he listens to the tape [with the victim story that he shares]. "I choke up", he shares, "I like [teaching 9/11] . . . I look forward to it." The facts and events of the day, and the impact on the victims, seem to be his focus, as opposed to larger historical events or concepts. For example, he shared that he does not particularly discuss terrorism as "they [the students] are aware of this". As with other teachers I interviewed, student and parent response seems to have been appreciative, to the extent that there was a response.

Another teacher said, "They [the students] need to understand this changed America—[it was a] huge paradigm shift". To help them internalize and deepen their understanding (beyond mere knowledge) of 9/11, now considered a necessary ingredient of patriotism, many teachers I spoke with share with students their own personal memories, though some were concerned that this would be too personal, too emotionally painful for them or would lead to accusations of being biased or political. Teacher 10 shared his story of the memory of watching 9/11 unfold, as so many of us did, on TV; he was a college student in his dorm at the time. Part of accomplishing this goal entails impressing upon students the depths of emotion that still surrounds 9/11. "They don't remember . . ." said Teacher 10, "they don't understand how a culture of fear took over".

## 78    9/11 and Collective Memory in U.S. Classrooms

As Teacher 2 said, "They need to see that an event like this was not just on TV." Teacher 9's sentiments were similar: "It's a really somber lesson". While every teacher I spoke with expressed feeling an obligation to pass on the memories of 9/11, a duty to teach their students to remember and honor the lives lost, it was no surprise that the history teachers in my study in particular felt so. Teacher 9 shared her own memories of 9/11: a college student at the time, she was geographically close enough to NYC that she "could see the smoke". She began saving newspaper coverage and in fact said that as a result, "I knew I was going to be a history teacher". She has invited guest speakers in from West Point speaking on counter-terrorism. In common with so many of her colleagues, Teacher 9 worked against the passage of time since 2001. Her students were seven or eight and, she said, "they remember a feeling" and recall "seeing tears" but without really knowing what had happened. To address this, she shows media coverage from September 2001 and asks each student to write down on an index card something they feel no one should forget about 9/11. Here of course we see another example of the definition of patriotism, at least among my participating teachers, I sketched out above. Patriotism in this activity means honoring and never forgetting the victims.

Teacher 7 said he considered teaching about 9/11 even more important than teaching about the three branches of government (though he was quick to assure interested parties that he of course does not neglect the Executive, Legislative nor the Judicial branch). Regarding 9/11, he said, "I wouldn't shortchange it for anything". He went on to express optimism about ultimate healing for Americans and even forgiveness: "Sooner or later people forgive and forget—I don't think this story should be forgotten."

Teacher 3's activities were a clear example of using 9/11 to teach the importance of patriotism. She had her middle schoolers make a large U.S. flag with values words such as "unity", "freedom" or "justice" written on it. Part of the perceived patriotism of teaching about 9/11 for many of the teachers I interviewed was designing an experience wherein the students could viscerally internalize the scope of gravity of the murder of nearly 3000 people. For Teacher 8, free writing was a means of accomplishing this. Upon being asked to reflect on 9/11, she said, her students would write about God, expressing gratitude for life "because you never know" (presumably suggesting that one never knows when one's own time will come). Being asked to reflect on 9/11 seemed to prompt her students to consider life's value and fragility. Despite the richness of her activities, this teacher also noted that she only addresses 9/11 once a year (on the memorial). She did add, however, that as an extra-curricular, she will periodically display material related to 9/11. She does so because "it's starting to fade". Such expressions are emblematic of grief and trauma; we struggle with the idea that if the memories fade, somehow the dead are dishonored. Is it possible for the pain to fade without the memories doing so? Collectively, this is to be hoped and worked for. We still seem to fear that if we let our collective

Educator Narratives of Teaching Terror   79

pain heal, we must therefore axiomatically let our guard down and therefore be made more vulnerable.

Teacher patriotism and generativity came through clearly as they spoke of a general concern for the next generation, and the desire to pass on specific values and identity narratives. As Teacher 2 evocatively phrase it, "You have to make it [9/11] a part of them." Again, the sense of the necessity of identification. The students, unless they are taught, she insisted, will not "know what patriotism is, they don't know what civil rights are." This is an especially disturbing thought given how under attack so many civil rights currently are, in ways directly related to 9/11. Consider for example recent revelations of the stunning extent of NSA surveillance both of Americans and foreigners, ally and enemy alike. Or consider the accusations of infiltration of mosques in New York City under Ray Kelly. His NYPD is currently being sued by the ACLU (Horwitz Online). This is an urgent moment in our history during which students are going to need knowledge of their rights!

Teacher 2 also referenced the fact that only twenty states out of our fifty current states mandate teaching about 9/11 as being "part of the problem". She expressed that teaching about 9/11 "is incredibly vital but you have to know what you're doing". Here Teacher 2 echoed the concerns of a number of her colleagues that I interviewed that many Americans, sometimes even teachers, do not necessarily have the command of all the facts needed to do the memory of 9/11 justice. She also noted that especially in the age of the internet, such misinformation can metastasize quickly. She felt this was a serious threat to the upcoming generation and their ability to take their place as adults in society when their time comes. "These kids are next," to lead society, as Teacher 2 noted, invoking the immense responsibility teachers have to support parents in preparing their kids for adulthood and the civic responsibility that comes with it.

Six of the twenty-four teachers shared that they had personally lost someone, or nearly so, as a result of 9/11. Teacher 2's relative became ill due to 9/11. Another had a relative who was a first responder. A third teacher with whom I sat down had served in the military. Yet a personal connection to that day was not necessary for a participant to express the sense that passing on the memories and knowledge of 9/11 is essential as an American—that we owe it to the dead. Nor was this sentiment always political or associated with the conservative politics that one might stereotypically expect. In fact, the majority of my teacher participants were firm that teachers must not take a political stand or even allow students to really know what sort of views they might have on a particular controversy related to 9/11, such as the occupation of Iraq or the use of torture to interrogate suspected terrorists. Similar to the professional stance of many journalists, these teachers feared being perceived as biased or, which seemed worse to some of the teachers I interviewed, somehow biasing the students. Along similar lines, some teachers feared (perhaps intuiting Volkan's theory of chosen trauma) passing on their own pain. Virtually each teacher I spoke

80  *9/11 and Collective Memory in U.S. Classrooms*

with had to grapple with this tight rope of truly (in an age-appropriate manner) teaching the terror of what occurred on 9/11—namely the murder of nearly 3000 civilians from over eighty countries—with concern for the impact of this information on their students. The complex and subjective question of what exactly "age appropriate" means also comes into play here; each educator has to make this judgment based on a knowledge of his or her own students. One teacher (in a science classroom) shares "not a lot" with her students about her own personal pain and memories; this was a teacher who could see the Twin Towers from her previous classroom in NYC. Some self-preservation is surely at work here as well. By contrast, another teacher suggested teachers should let their students see the emotion and pain of discussing 9/11 as a part of the educational experience. Teacher 2 felt her 8th graders were not yet ready for the political issues involved with teaching about 9/11 but was adamant that they needed to know the facts.

Teacher 4, like her colleagues, worked to instill in her students what she perceives to be a patriotic view of 9/11. As she noted, her history club presents a power point to "remind people of the event" and to "honor our service men and women who are our protectors." This teacher brought in a first responder (a fire fighter) who had been present on 9/11. As one would imagine, "the kids were pretty entranced with him". This particular teacher had a student who was killed during 9/11 and so the personal connection of a particular teacher to the attacks that took place on 9/11 inspired a commitment to pass the knowledge on to students.

For Teacher 16, the notion of patriotism was fraught and complex (as I find it to be myself, in such a militarized age). She shared her concern about the "rather inflammatory and anti-Muslim" narrative she thinks students are getting. Her context seems important here; she is in AZ, which like CO and TX, has experienced conservative backlash against multi-cultural curriculum as unpatriotic. (The racist implication of this backlash is that America is fundamentally white and Christian.) I was fascinated by her observation that her Hispanic American students in particular, whom she describes as being "very aware of their status as second-class citizens", have a different perspective on 9/11 than her white students. They, she explains, "look at 9/11 in a totally different way—they connect with a different part of the experience". She hesitated some here, surely conscious of not wanting to perpetuate the narrative of non-white Americans as somehow less loyal or less fully American.

Others expressed feeling a sense of duty to teach about 9/11 given its towering significance in our history. Teacher Twelve observed that 9/11 "is so prevalent in how Americans perceive themselves". As an educator who aspires to foster values of peace and justice in her classroom, she expressed regret at her initial view of 9/11 that America had probably deserved it. She was living overseas at the time, she detailed, and did not have enough compassion for the ordinary Americans who had so suddenly and so violently lost a loved one. It simply took her some more time, she reflected, to "grow

*Educator Narratives of Teaching Terror* 81

up". She believes that teaching about 9/11 fostered more humility and compassion in her. Like many of her colleagues participating in this research, she seems to try to design an emotional experience for her students for an understanding of 9/11 that goes beyond the intellectual. To the extent that she overtly emphasizes patriotism, she emphasizes "the pride and heroism of that day" and aims to help students understand both the geographical and historical context which conspired to make 9/11 a reality. She was concerned that students are "aging out" of having their own personal memories of 9/11. She also clearly desired for her students' "kind" of patriotism to be of an informed, thoughtful and critical kind. For example, while she shows the documentary "Inside 9/11" to foster an affective connection with the events of that day, she had concerns about what she felt was an uncritical kind of patriotism in this documentary that, in her view, misrepresented in particular the invasion and occupation of Iraq. She worried that the documentary "acts like Iraq was an appropriate response when it was not". She insists on teaching about 9/11, despite its absence from her curriculum, due to her conviction that it simply is too consequential to U.S. and world events to neglect. She also said her students express a lot of curiosity about 9/11 and so has a sense of responsibility to them as well as the related responsibilities to country and history.

Teacher 2 used the phrase "defining moment" and noted that "so many things changed after that [9/11] in our history". Teacher 4 expressed a similar observation: "As time goes on we'll have students who weren't alive." Teacher 4 expressed the desire to "help students grow in the understanding", explaining, "that's just who I am." She related teaching about 9/11 to other central events in modern U.S. history, such as the assassination of JFK. These are simply things one must know to function as an American. Virtually every teacher I interviewed expressed this sentiment—that we have a duty to pass the memories of that day on to the next generation. Teacher 2 elaborated some more: she speaks to her students (on 9/11 and during other lessons throughout the year which she connects to 9/11) about heroism, prompting consideration of who might merit that term, who acted heroically on 9/11 and of course how students can aspire to that character.

This patriotic commitment to teaching about 9/11 led Teacher 3 to approach the administration to continue school-wide programs on the anniversary of 9/11. This was especially important to her as a former member of the military. She recalls having "gone full out" to teach about 9/11 in 2002, concerned that if she did not, no one else would. She was not able to interest her administration in a planned guest speaker or assembly or similar activity (though she does recall for the first couple of years after 2001, a moment of silence was held). The barrier of time, given the political choices we make about what is and is not important enough to devote time to in the classroom, is evident here.

Teacher 19 shared the desire of most of his colleagues to impress upon students the pain, confusion and fear of 9/11. "I want the kids to think

## 82  9/11 and Collective Memory in U.S. Classrooms

about the feelings—I will always take with me the feelings" associated with 9/11. A main goal of his memorial lesson seems to be conveying the intensity. He shares with his students that nearly 20% of the school went home the day of 9/11 (again, this is a school somewhat close in proximity to Manhattan so many parents came to pick up their kids). He shares a further personal story with his students, addressing the challenge of trying to teach a subject as intense and complex as 9/11 at the beginning of the school year (without much time to yet build community) by using the discussion itself as an icebreaker. "I share with them," he says, "I share with them what it was like (on 9/11) in our building". As it happened, a fellow teacher across the hall had a relative she thought might be in Tower 7. Naturally she was panicked when she could not reach anyone on her cell as the entire network was down. We all recall where we were when the first plane hit the first Tower; Teacher 19, like myself, was in his classroom. Fortunately his planning period was when the attack itself occurred and he narrates for his students that "you could feel a seismic shift in the building—you could feel it, everyone was out of the classrooms going 'what's going on?'" He "wanted to grab [his] kids and go hide", as he shares with the class. In addition to the above, he shares with students the moment when he says the historical significance of 9/11 "really hit me". He was coaching his soccer team when he and his players heard a "thunderous noise" overhead. He and all of his kids were looking up, watching the sky. As it happened the plane was Air Force One transporting then President Bush from New York to Washington, DC. This scene reminded me of my own similar experience (related in Chapter 1) of seeing a small plane fly entirely too close to the Washington Monument and then noticing everyone else with me on the National Mall that day watching the plane just as I had been.

A final vignette Teacher 19 shares sometimes with students, in an attempt to personalize it for them and convey the human reality of what occurred, was precipitated by the simple act of hanging laundry out on the line in his back yard. He lives near a PA airport, and so the attendant background noise is constant. As he hung his laundry he realized how silent it was, as all air traffic in the entire country was still grounded, and understood "at that point the world was different—it would never be the same". Of course he becomes emotional relating these stories but is confident that "the kids understand" and even "appreciate it when teachers are not afraid to personalize things". Indeed, the affective domain, as peace educators have long stressed, is essential for creating classroom community and humanizing the Other.

From the perspective of collective narratives, then, and their potential impact on war and peace, the question becomes: how is patriotism defined, expressed and taught (both explicitly and as a part of the hidden curriculum) in U.S. classrooms? What is the impact of a moment of silence if students scarcely comprehend the reason for it? If there is a void in education about 9/11, as my data suggests that there is, from where do students gather puzzle pieces to form some sort of narrative about 9/11 and its meaning for the U.S. and the world? From airports where they must take their shoes off before getting on a plane? Ahistorical documentaries like CNN's recent call to "Find the Flag" (there was even a hashtag ready-made for twitter!) or Hollywood versions of 9/11 such as Nick Cage's *World Trade Center?* While few would disagree with presenting FDNY first responders as heroes of 9/11, this movie focuses its thin plot entirely on the horror of two specific firemen trapped in the Towers during an attempted rescue, and the subsequent (successful) attempts to rescue them in turn. Most of the movie takes place in the Tower itself, or in the homes and with the families of the two trapped men. The plot offers virtually nothing about any sort of history regarding 9/11; perhaps the writers assume this is not necessary. Its purpose is primarily to be an action-adventure rescue drama. Its purpose with respect to plot clearly seems to be redemptive. Other documentaries feature news coverage from the day itself, and subsequent interviews with survivors and first responders. We have virtually no pop-culture portrayal of American Muslims to speak of (except perhaps an episode of Morgan Spurlock's "30 Days" during which he spent thirty days living with a Muslim American family). The CW's "Aliens in America", a family sit-com about a high school boy from Pakistan who comes to live with a white American family, was short lived. A TLC show, "All American Muslim", looking to depict an average American Muslim family, was quickly cancelled in controversy during 2012 ("TLC cancels" online). As of this writing, Marvel comics just announced a new young Muslim girl (Kamala Khan, a Pakistani immigrant to New Jersey) to their collection of superheroes, perhaps beginning to fill the void (Khan online).

This all leads again to broader questions of how American identity itself is depicted in the classroom. Is its complexity and diversity represented? More specifically, is the narrative of 9/11 being passed on one which leaves space for healing or one which will perpetuate chosen trauma? This largely appears to depend on the approach of the teacher. Parents, teachers, students and Americans in general need to know that a complex, historically-grounded, multifaceted narrative about 9/11 is, based on my data, the exception in American classrooms, and not the rule. With enough determination, a teacher can present a comprehensive, historically grounded and contextualized understanding of 9/11 (the event and metaphor, not just the day) but this entails overcoming some very real barriers. We will examine those barriers in more detail shortly.

## 9/11 AS A LESSON IN CRITICAL THINKING: "I WANT THEM TO COME TO THEIR OWN EDUCATED CONCLUSIONS"

Critical thinking was a final, and predominant, theme from my teacher interviews. In my view, here is much hope for education in the U.S.— if teachers, parents and indeed students themselves keep insisting that

## 84  *9/11 and Collective Memory in U.S. Classrooms*

educational policy makers do not continue to narrow curricular space for creativity and critical engagement in the classroom. The troubling trend now is just such a narrowing, but I did find impressive examples of especially experienced teachers finding ways around testing-driven reforms to ensure that critical thought and engagement remain alive in their classrooms. While we cannot pretend that the lessons and curriculum described below are typical, they do represent spaces of some sort of limited autonomy for teachers as public intellectuals. As importantly, they represent potential spaces of praxis for students. Critical peace pedagogy of course has long argued for how essential such spaces are if we are to continually expand and deepen our democracy.

History, government and literature are perhaps the easiest disciplines to connect to teaching 9/11, yet my research also generated examples of math and science teachers creatively connecting their subject to 9/11. One teacher used her science curriculum to teach students about the science of disaster response, the structural engineering of buildings to withstand impact (be it from an attack or a natural event) and the health impacts that first responders experienced as a result of the smoke inhalation, air quality in New York City and DC after the attacks, chemicals from clean up and physical and emotional stress of having to be so long at Ground Zero. Tectonic plates and comparative disaster response also feature into her lesson, as she reviews differing approaches from around the world. Interestingly, she noted to me that she feels certain safety corners were cut with regard to our response to 9/11, and she brings this into the discussion as well. Such discussions challenge student critical thinking and are consistent with the principles of peace education. In this case specifically, this teacher's approach fosters students' ability to understand the application of science for meeting basic human needs. Relatedly, she emphasizes to her students that "the power of science can be very destructive", creating a teachable moment to model and foster ethical reasoning in her students.

Teacher 8 exemplified an emphasis on critical thinking. An English teacher of mostly high school seniors, she described herself as having large classes with mostly Hispanic and African American students and outdated access to technology (while she has a computer herself, there is no smart board, only a chalk board, and there are no computers for the students). She offers an entire "mini-unit", even though it is not formally a part of the curriculum, on critical thinking at the beginning of the year. This unit includes differing philosophies of right and wrong and how to go about ethical reasoning (like Kant for example). She also uses this unit to introduce her students to the logical fallacies. In this way, she feels they become more prepared for the discussions to come throughout the year, be it literature or 9/11. When it comes time to teach about 9/11 itself, Teacher 8 uses the opportunity to involve students in thinking about what sort of boundaries and community standards are appropriate for such a controversial and painful topic. This engages student critical and ethical reasoning as they have to consider where reasonable community standards for behavior end and censorship or infringements on free speech begin. This is a vital skill for citizenship in a democracy. Apparently this emerged out of Teacher 8's reflective practice after some specific students made some inappropriate comments. She shared in particular that one student had announced, "I'm glad they're dead" regarding the victims of 9/11.

Teacher 8 is also able to use the differences between her own views of foreign policy (which lean more liberal) and the views of her students (which are more conservative) to create teachable moments and critical dialogues. She feels free (in contrast to some of the other teachers I interviewed) to share her liberal views with her students. As she tells it, they feel free to tease her about them and share their more right-leaning views. She explains, "I would never take points off" for a particular view a student expressed, "only for logical fallacies". She reports that the students seem to understand this and "are pretty good natured" regarding their political differences (between herself and the students and within the student body). Her students "see the U.S. as the victim" of 9/11, and "they don't concede that we could be at fault or could have done something differently". She works through her discussion to complicate and nuance this view. I was especially impressed by this as it destabilizes the founding myth of U.S. innocence which impedes critical thinking as regards our history. Teacher 8 also seems to have benefitted from some leadership regarding teaching about 9/11 by her principal. One year he sent along a William Safire article for them to use. Relatedly she has not ever experienced anyone suggesting that she avoid certain topics or not teach about 9/11 at all. She was clear on this: "I've never run into any problems whatsoever. . . . I've never had anyone say 'you can't do that'". As a veteran teacher who has been in the classroom since 1989, she seems to have developed the confidence and skill needed to navigate tricky curricular territory. Much of this seems to flow from the relationships and community she is able to develop with her students. She is able to discuss some of the most difficult and divisive issues emerging from 9/11 with her students (again, mostly juniors and seniors in her English class). She and her students typically disagree on torture and on the invasion of Iraq (it is useful to remember here many students seem to have the misconception that Iraq was responsible for 9/11). "We disagree," she states, "the vast majority of kids think torture is fine". Despite the strong relationships, she said, "they do get upset with me, for some reason they make that jump to Iraq". At this point, she has to "refresh their memory about WMD". What a teachable moment this is! Here is an opportunity for students to be introduced to critical media theory! It was no mistake that kids "jump to Iraq"—there was a campaign of disinformation and propaganda by our government which precipitated this misconception.

Like Teacher 8, Teacher 10 was also deliberate and intentional regarding the inclusion of critical thinking in her unit on 9/11. She focuses them on the role of the media, for example, emphasizing the need for multiple

## 86 9/11 and Collective Memory in U.S. Classrooms

sources of information. "What is media," she asks them, framing the lesson, "and how does it affect our culture?" This desire to inspire her students to think critically appears to be in tension, however, with another desire expressed by Teacher 10, which is the desire to be seen as unbiased and avoid trouble. As she said, "You have to make sure you're not pushing an agenda". Most of all, Teacher 10 wanted her students to understand and reflect critically on how much the U.S. had changed in reaction to 9/11. To help them understand, she relates to her students her own story of experiencing 9/11 as a college fresher. Like a number of her colleagues, she gave her students what has emerged as the most popular assignment to be given according to the teachers I interviewed: asking students to interview or dialogue with someone at home about their first-hand memories. The students type up their interviews and blog them (she has the fortune to be in a classroom where each kid has his or her own laptop). She noted that this activity made it necessary for her to be "very open" to whatever the students might return to the classroom with as she "didn't know what they would bring to the table". She expressed her students' enthusiasm for the assignment: "the kids have so many great questions! You have no idea!" She moves about the classroom as students type up and share the blogs describing their interviews. A salutary result of this interaction is the opportunity it affords her to correct misinformation or lack of information that students commonly have. For example, some of her students had never heard of Bin Laden. As in other classrooms, some of her students believed that Iraq had attacked the U.S. on 9/11. This blogging activity also allows her to collaborate with other teachers (she currently partners with Teacher 9) to enable students to read different perspectives on 9/11 from another part of the country, dialoging student to student online.

This teacher's self-reflection and self-critique impressed me. Lamenting the outdated nature of her textbooks, which mention neither 9/11 nor the 1994 genocide in Rwanda, she considered the difficulty of providing the full historical context which students need to understand 9/11. Afghanistan, she said, "comes up a little bit" and she reports that she gives students a bit of the relevant history but does not fully address the war itself in Afghanistan. When I asked why not, she reported, "our school is really liberal or really conservative". This is a clear example of the sort of self-censorship that we educators find ourselves engaging in. She further detailed that, for example, she does not mention to her students that her fiancé is a veteran. "I don't want them to think," she disclosed, "that I'm all for war". It seems there is some context shaping her choices. "Other teachers have had really bad things—I mean, not bad but parent complaints" regarding how teachers in her district were teaching about 9/11. I gather a parent felt one of the district's teachers was "telling kids it's bad to go to war" which offended this parent, who was a veteran. For this reason, Teacher 10 explained, "when it is controversial I give the kids a choices project". In this manner, a student who does not want to engage does not have too. She also noted that as a result of the apparent controversies, "a reminder always goes out around 9/11 to be careful". The chilling effect on a critical academic environment, let alone the ability to realize critical peace education, becomes clear in such teacher narratives. We remember from Chapter 3 that, quantitatively speaking, most teachers felt academically safe when teaching about 9/11. Further, recall that only a very small percentage of teachers reported that they had experienced explicitly "hostile" reactions to their curriculum, be it from colleagues, students, administrators or the community. Yet I have been positing the reality behind these numbers reveals of various kinds of self-censorship. Some of this is reasonably benign in considering students' ages, especially in middle school (as in not wanted to show actual footage of the planes hitting the Towers or people jumping out of them or concern that a class discussion of 9/11 would reveal that a student in the class had suffered a personal loss due to the attacks). Teachers taking care of ourselves emotionally, and respecting our own limits when it comes to personally painful topics, is likewise understandable. Other aspects of self-censorship by those of us in the classroom (and I—again—do not consider myself entirely an exception) need more critical self-reflection by the entire profession. What is the impact of teachers avoiding certain controversial subjects? Or not bringing certain views into the classroom for fear of backlash? Do we truly serve students by laboring to be neutral? Policy makers, administrators, teachers, parents and students alike must prize robust debate, rather than fearing the possible legal or other consequences. This will mean a fundamental shift in how we view teachers and schools.

Teachers used activities like class debate, reflective writing and group discussion, among others, to foster critical analysis and critical thinking regarding why 9/11 occurred and what the U.S. response was/should have been. As one teacher noted, "students know what happened from the media, but don't know why". Teachers also consistently expressed concern about the internet as a source for student learning about 9/11, rife as it is with conspiracy theories. At least two teachers specifically facilitated debate about the killing of Bin Laden. Others asked students to consider the invasion of Iraq and Afghanistan, or the use of torture. We were grappling with the dilemma of neutrality above; these teachers, while they did not tend to share with students their own views, did directly bring the controversies into their classroom for students to consider and debate. As one teacher phrased it, "I do have a passion about events that caused our policy to change direction." She, like many Americans, perceived 9/11 to have precipitated responses that are unwise and she is dedicated to inspiring students to think critically and reflect deeply. For her the significance of 9/11 pedagogically was that "it was a defining moment in our history, so many things changed after that." She feels strongly that students should be guided to ask questions about our response to 9/11, how others view the U.S., what patriotism means, and what justice looks like.

88   *9/11 and Collective Memory in U.S. Classrooms*

While she did not "blame America" for 9/11, Teacher 6 on the other hand did state clearly that "we [the U.S.] were accountable and culpable for 9/11 in very serious ways." She brings into her class several graphs that compare deaths resulting from 9/11 to deaths caused by U.S. wars "in pursuit of oil" as she put it. Anticipating perhaps the controversial nature of this statement, she wanted me to know that as someone originally from Brooklyn, on the day of 9/11, she herself picked up impacted friends who were "covered in dust" from the attacks. In her words: "Even if you lost someone, as an educator, you have a responsibility to think critically". Despite this traumatic memory, she views it as a professional duty to engage students in critical thinking about painful issues (as age appropriate). Said Teacher 6, "As a teacher you shouldn't be having an emotional response, you should have kids doing critical thinking." Notably this continued the pattern of some teachers who responded to my call for participants having had some sort of personal connection to the events of 9/11. She specifically wanted her students to consider power dynamics related to U.S. history, world history and 9/11. She connects the events of 9/11 to other sorts of injustice, which for her would include the status of Native Americans, migrant workers and colonialism. Drones are a focus of the dialogue that she facilitates. Given how colonialism and the dictatorial regimes post-colonialism have dominated Middle East politics, this is a useful connection for students to make. For her, patriotism is about the diversity of Americans, with our proud and painful history, continuing to perfect our union. "We get," she explained, "to a really beautiful place of equity . . . and a much clearer perspective of ourselves" as a result of these classroom discussions focused on power, privilege, history and social justice. Teacher 6 refers to this approach as "backwards thinking", that is, examining a current event in history and then walking "backwards" in history to understand the current event's context, past history and causes.

Further building on this theme of critical thinking, she relates her lessons on 9/11 to what she views as a national culture that glorifies violence. In particular, she invites her students to consider the glorification of violence and "militarism" in Hollywood. Connecting this specifically to 9/11, she asks students to study and consider the killing of Bin Laden, as well as the subsequent reactions of celebration. She conflicted with the "male administration" at her previous school when she raised the question of whether or not the killing of Bin Laden was just. One objective, she explained, was teaching her boys in particular to "pull back from the tendency towards bravado". She was the only teacher I spoke with who directly linked militarism and patriarchy. This teacher's worldview seemed to assume that education is naturally going to be uncomfortable at times and that if we are to do right by our students and our society, we must accept this.

With a very small Muslim population in her school and community, Teacher 6 had a particular concern about dangerous stereotypes and what the field of conflict resolution would call enemy images of Muslims. "It's disgusting," she said, to think that the first images most of her students had of Islam was that they "kill babies" and are "stinky bombers". Here she uses the previously mentioned "backwards thinking" strategy of framing the discussion around two main critical thinking questions: what occurred relevant to an event in history? Next, "walking back" in history, what had happened before that might explain our current situation? This helps her students, she explains, gain an understanding of history "from the perspective of the Other". Her language suggests an obvious versing in critical pedagogy theory. She was the one (out of twenty-four) teachers I interviewed who explicitly employed such language from critical theory.

Another key aspect of this teacher's curriculum, in accord with critical theory, is encouraging her students to question the official government narrative about 9/11. She does this via structured discussion and research activities regarding the U.S. role in the world in general. Regarding 9/11 specifically, she designs a "fact/opinion" chart which she reports helps students to organize and clarify their thinking with respect to what we know and do not know about the events of that day. This, she feels, is particularly important since her students enter her classroom having "heard the rhetoric, they hear these terrible things from television . . . rhetoric is floating around society in very damaging ways." Without facts and the critical thinking skills necessary to sort through all of the propaganda and rhetoric, students will of course not be in a position to understand if, when and how they are being mislead or manipulated.

She even introduces the questions which some have raised around "Building 7", which also collapsed on 9/11. Some structural engineers have suggested that the manner in which it collapsed suggest that explosives were the cause, contradicting the official report (see the documentary *9/11: Explosive Evidence—Experts Speak Out*, which aired on PBS). This narrative has not gained much traction, but Teacher 6 brings it into her classroom despite her concern about the controversy. "I don't want to be accused of indoctrination", she says. In response to these accusations, she says, "I don't ever really come to conclusions with my kids but it allows them to be thoughtful". Consistent with the other teachers that I interviewed, she continues: "I want them to come to their own educated conclusions". She feels this grounding in historical context is especially important when teaching about painful or traumatic events like 9/11 since it is precisely those events which are the most charged with emotions for students and teachers alike and hence the most difficult for us as human beings to think clearly about.

Teacher 6 was similar to the others I spoke with in this respect. Far and away, the most serious concern teachers I spoke with had when it comes to navigating 9/11 in the classroom is the concern that someone would think them biased or trying to push a political agenda, even indoctrinating the students. Her response to this is a conceptual building block of critical pedagogy, which is to remind critics that there is no such thing as a neutral perspective. They simply do not exist. To remain "neutral" then is to

## 90 *9/11 and Collective Memory in U.S. Classrooms*

reproduce the status quo. In her own words: "every teacher has an agenda and if they say they don't, that's dishonest". Or as Howard Zinn was fond of saying, "You can't be neutral on a moving train!"

This theme of wanting to teach reflection and critical thinking skills is where much of the frustration with a regimented and test-driven curriculum emerged. Frustration with being limited to state standards was especially clear of the history teachers who spoke with me, as one might imagine. One teacher even remarked that were it left solely to state curriculum standards and textbooks, students would never get past the Vietnam War. (As a high school history student, I never got past WWII.) They more than their colleagues teaching other subjects, as one might expect, felt the most free to delve into the history behind and current events controversies emerging from the attacks on 9/11. One teacher, for example, integrated teaching about 9/11, and the U.S. response, to previous wars fought in U.S. history, such as Vietnam. Teachers also seemed concerned to impress upon students, as one might imagine, the terrible import of 9/11 for the U.S. Teachers mentioned Pearl Harbor repeatedly in comparison to 9/11, as is also the case in most media reflection of the event. These reflections tend to observe that 9/11 was the first time since Pearl Harbor that America had suffered an attack on its own soil. Being immune from at least direct attack had almost become part and parcel of American Exceptionalism until 9/11.

A number of teachers, but especially the history and English teachers I spoke with, used personal reflective writing to facilitate students connecting with and comprehending the events of 9/11. Teacher 15 employed an online discussion board her school hosted to facilitate a brief discussion on the day of 9/11. Most recently she focused the discussion on the image of what has come to be called "Falling Man", the male silhouette used, or referenced, in various documentaries and coverage of 9/11, to include *60 Minutes*. Falling Man was a controversial photo taken on 9/11 that depicted a man, seemingly serene in his suit, as he fell upside-down towards the concrete, having jumped from one of the Towers.

As a means of engaging student critical thinking, she invites students to consider (as the media had to do) what images were appropriate and what was not. This opened online and some classroom discussion of the events of 9/11 themselves. She also invites a guest speaker in who has created a graphic novel about 9/11. The students were given a chance to ask the artist questions, which Teacher 15 reported were primarily about the publication process rather than 9/11 itself. Students, she said, welcomed the activities and discussion about 9/11 whether it was in the formal curriculum or not. They would tell her, as she explained, "I was afraid to ask" or express to her, "I never really knew what happened".

Teacher 7's unique approach one year involved students engaging local community members in interviews. They gathered oral histories from people on their experiences and memories of 9/11. He considered this particularly important for his students as they are located in the Midwest and so geographically rather removed from the events of 9/11. Along these lines, he also makes use of google earth to allow students to virtually "visit" Ground Zero and see the year-by-year reconstruction. Given the importance, gravity and complexity of the subject, he says he was resistant to the idea of simply giving kids a worksheet, given his objective of fostering critical thinking. He reports that "the kids understood it, were interested, ran with it". Based on his interaction and experience with the students, he believes the students have a "collective memory" (his phrase) of 9/11 and that they need an opportunity to explore those memories. Giving them this opportunity to gather oral histories and make meaning around 9/11 is essential, he believes. Student engagement and enthusiasm resulted in such success, as he reports it, that everyone received and A+ for the project! This even attracted some media attention. The *Washington Post* sent a reporter who Teacher 7 said "lambasted" the town and students most unfairly. While he witnessed much student success and passion for the project, the reporter put in a story about how local students did not know or care about 9/11. He even shared that the reporter got a picture of one student's shoes and claimed the kids cared more about fashion than 9/11. He felt this reporter "came into town with the story written". Other more local media coverage of his unit was much more favorable and in his view accurate. This perhaps crystalizes part of the emergent collective narrative about 9/11—the fear of it being forgotten by forthcoming generations.

Like many of the other educators who spoke with me, Teacher 7 worked to involve students in a thoughtful and critical discussion of U.S. political and social culture and our national response to Sept 11. He, quite boldly in my view, asks kids if they would have the courage to "get on an airplane for their religious beliefs". Powerful questions like this not only provoke healthy democratic debate ("can you consider a terrorist courageous? What makes someone a terrorist? Why would someone do such a thing to innocent people they'd never met?") but also open essential space from a peace education perspective for the development of critical consciousness. Such questions are salutary in that they destabilize current extremist narratives about the world's Muslims and open some space for a narrative that is more three-dimensional, historical and humanized. Emblematic of his concerns about lack of knowledge (including his own) about Muslims, and a lack of contact and dialogue, he related a story to me about an Iranian American who lived near him during the time of the hostage crisis in 1978/9. He asked his neighbor about the Shah but this seems to have been one of his only opportunities for direct dialogue with a Muslim. He noted to me that he appreciates the movie *Flight 93* for this reason, as in his view it presented the hijackers in a three-dimensional manner. They "had a motive, it was a cause they honestly believed in". He was sure to note to students in addition that historically speaking, Christians have also turned to political violence.

Teacher 7 like virtually all of his colleagues was concerned with students absorbing inaccurate historical information: "they've seen too much

## 92   *9/11 and Collective Memory in U.S. Classrooms*

History Channel or Oliver Stone". Regarding the development of empathy, Teacher 7 also expressed his concern not only about stereotypes of Muslims but about an immunity in U.S. culture to violence in general. "Sometimes you get so immune to things", he said. He related this observation to numbness (even for himself as a teacher or among his students) resulting from "media overload". His framing was to pose to students the question of which to them is more important—protection from wrongful search and seizure or ensuring that we never again experience another attack like the one that took place on 9/11. "That's a hard question to answer", he concedes. So it is, and we as a nation have struggled with it since 9/12/01. His question elicits some telling responses from students; one reportedly asked him, "Why am I doing this [having to take off one's shoes or have one's laptop scanned]—I don't look like a terrorist—I don't look Middle Eastern." Clearly this student had absorbed the Islamophobia that has been so prevalent in our political culture since 9/11 (and indeed before). Interestingly, the subject of Islam itself has not come up, according to Teacher 7. When I asked why he thought this was, he suggested it was due to the demographics of his classroom and school community which is 98% Christian. His own confidence in the subject matter also seemed to pose an issue. As Teacher 7 related, "if you were to ask me what the tenants of Islam are, I frankly can't tell you". There are no Mosques or synagogues nearby. How in such a context does one facilitate student encounters of the Other?

As a history teacher, he works to put 9/11 in historical perspective by for example asking students what they know about WWII's kamikaze pilots. He conceded that he does not know much about the Patriot Act but "tries to show the kids two sides of the debate". This lack of background knowledge and/or lack of confidence in one's readiness to address all of the relevant issues that ought to be part of a complete and challenging unit on 9/11, to include some of the history of the Cold War, South East Asian and Middle Eastern history, U.S. constitutional issues, Islamic theology, Islamophobia and so on is a real barrier. Teacher 6 spoke to this barrier as well quite frankly: "I meet more ignorant teachers than I do kids". This speaks again to the need for training, time and space for teacher professional development.

For some teachers I interviewed, fostering critical thinking through teaching about 9/11 meant delving with students into the historical context of 9/11. This entailed, as Teacher 4, Teacher 6 and Teacher 16 in particular described, teaching about the Cold War, the Soviet invasion of Afghanistan, and of course events related to the U.S. response to 9/11, such as the U.S. occupation of Afghanistan, the PATRIOT Act, the invasion of Iraq and other similar developments. Ensuring comprehensive student understanding, as Teacher 4 said, also involved plenty of background on the features of the U.S. government. Teacher 4 provided information on key concepts such as various freedoms guaranteed in the Bill of Rights, the separation of powers key to maintaining our freedom, and what powers the

## Educator Narratives of Teaching Terror 93

Constitution does in fact give the President. For Teacher 4, the invasions and occupations of Iraq and Afghanistan were a real-time lesson in "how the President and the Congress negotiate". This related especially to the national debates Americans had regarding war powers or the use of torture during interrogation of suspected terrorists and if and how to close Guantanamo Bay. Like the strong majority of teachers, Teacher 4 worked hard to not reveal personal opinions or biases. S/he wanted students to debate the issues themselves, though apparently the confidence of the students in their debate skills was somewhat of a barrier to this goal. Confidence, of course, comes with experience and time. She reported that, much like the adults in America, her students were fairly divided on the issue of using torture.

Another teacher (Teacher 21) offered her students a personal reflection of her own to foster critical thinking—that she used to be able to go to dinner at the [city name withheld] airport. Of course this is no longer possible. She then invites them to compare and contrast (a common critical thinking standard in many state curricula) things we as Americans could do before that we cannot do now. She also leads a discussion about the "dehumanization of Islam and 9/11. Questions like do we trust people are asked". This teacher, though she has not yet implemented this, is considering for next year Document Based Questions (DBQ), which entails "looking at both sides and then asking questions about the two points of view and then having the student do research and answer the questions". While not experiential in comparison to other possible activities, such an approach does engage students in grappling intellectually with different historical narratives.

Teacher 10 also used classroom dialogue, a documentary which challenged harmful stereotypes about Muslims, as well as community connections to engage students in critical thinking about 9/11. Like several other teachers I spoke with, she gave students an assignment to interview an adult older enough to have clear memories of 9/11. She reports that "the parents loved it" and the students would return to class with powerful and vivid stories to share. Furthering the connections with a community outside the classroom, the students then type up the interviews in a set of blog entries.

A central theme of this book is that 9/11 is a collective event, experienced by individuals both personally and as members of various identity groups. So it seemed very fitting that two teachers I spoke with (both history and U.S. government teachers) collaborated on a unit involving social media to enable their students to interact with other students in different parts of the country to share memories, views and make meaning around 9/11. Teachers 9 and 10 in particular coordinated with one another such that their students could read one another's blogs and comment in response. When teachers take this sort of risk and engage students in meaningful connections and dialogue, the students often reward it with investment and quality work. Not merely answering but learning to *ask* questions is an important component of critical thinking at the high school level. Such

## 94  9/11 and Collective Memory in U.S. Classrooms

activities do involve some risk for teachers as one never knows, and cannot control, what stories and emotions students will return to the classroom with. As Teacher 10 said, "[You have to be] very open—I didn't know what they would bring to the table". Indeed, I would argue that a certain amount of risk and de-centering the teacher, which will always entail a loss of control, is necessary for a vibrant classroom. This ethos, needless to say, is the antithesis of the standards movement.

Teacher 11 similarly used engaging activities to inspire students to think critically about the events and meaning of 9/11. Formally she addresses 9/11 on the memorial date only but engages the subject when students bring it up in relation to other historical topics and reported that sometimes, she is not able to address 9/11 even on the date of commemoration. She has sometimes used "102 Minutes that Changed America" to help students learn the basics and finds herself, like so many other teachers addressing 9/11, correcting misinformation and countering conspiracy theories. Other activities in her classroom include providing students with a list of documentaries on 9/11 and asking them to write a response to one of them. For the 10th Anniversary Memorial lesson, she had her students access the Smithsonian website to explore the artifacts and narratives there. She then provides a set of newspapers and magazines which had coverage of 9/11. From there students were prepared to design their own 9/11 Memorial Museum, writing about what they would include and why. The next step was collaborative and fostered collective meaning-making; students were asked to respond to one another's museums. Metacognition was the final step, as students were asked to reflect on what the activities helped them understand about 9/11 and why.

Teacher 16 focused students on a central dilemma of every society: "How do you maintain a free society and secure yourself?" She guides her students to reflect on what they would—or would not—sacrifice for a free society and lamented to me that some of her students, especially the white ones, were "totally willing to trade any freedom we have for a sense of security". She works to inform and complicate their "pretty simplistic" views about the history of what happened on 9/11 and why. The common student narrative (and the common narrative overall, one could argue) was that "the U.S. was both the victim and the hero and then we kicked some butt in Afghanistan". It is not denial of the heroism of first responders, or the victimhood of those who perished on 9/11 and their surviving loved ones to recognize that the story, indeed any story, is more complex than that. Filling out the narrative, challenging its simplicity, is essential to what Sara Cobb (2013) calls a "better-formed story", without which narrative peace building cannot occur. Teacher 16's further reflections spoke to just this point. She actually had students, in the context of such discussion, ask her, "Are we allowed to think this?" She would assure them that "the only thing that is un-American is to suppress our speech". She, like other teachers who successfully navigated these sorts of charged conversations with

# Educator Narratives of Teaching Terror    95

students, feels that she was able to do so due to having established trust and credibility in classroom. She would tell them they were free to have whatever point of view they liked, so long as they argued from evidence and she was able to make them feel respected even when they disagreed. She valued such opportunities to model in her classroom what civil democratic debate should look like. This was, I think, especially valuable in her local context, where as she reports, "social studies teachers are regularly crucified" in local media for not teaching "right-wing conservative values".

Teacher 24, at a private school in upstate NY, used the (in my view excellent) *Facing History and Ourselves* curriculum to teach his interdisciplinary global studies and humanities course. (What a delight to have a participating teacher whose curriculum and school set-up was explicitly interdisciplinary!) When teaching about 9/11, he draws on their curriculum regarding terrorism to "talk about realities, emotional reactions, history, community". He reports that "things get sensitive and hard but then we go into the history of the Middle East and we look at the series 'Why Do They Hate Us?'". This discussion is meant to help students process, reflect, engage critically and have the historical context to understand 9/11 and the U.S. policy responses to it. Teacher 24 perceived that this approach has been successful: "The reactions are tremendously positive from both students and parents because this is all within the context of the broad curricula of our school". With the greater academic, curricular and pedagogical flexibility afforded by a private school, he need not worry about restricting himself to a day or matching each lesson activity to a particular state learning standard. (I myself can recall writing VA SOL standard numbers on the white board in my middle/high school literature and writing classrooms next to each agenda item as though this somehow demonstrated effectiveness or accountability.) Perhaps due to this flexibility, he continued describing his approach as one where "discussions center on students and not on teachers". This means much of his methodology was based on listening "to [student] divergent issues" and in particular helping students to try to understand and process the fear many of them have absorbed as a result of growing up in the post-9/11 era. He also expressed his concern that critical thinking is not sufficiently engaged in most curricular approaches to teaching about 9/11 and the resulting danger of continuing conflict if the narrative is not interrupted and improved. He worried that teaching 9/11 too often became about either "patriotism or anti-imperialism" when in his view "teaching 9/11 should be about opening a broad conversation in a broad way, into the complexity of those issues, and not be narrowed down to an event, but open up space for a bigger conversation". He clearly intends his pedagogy to foster increased critical thinking, dialogue and understanding.

Perhaps inevitably, while every teacher I spoke with valued critical thinking, at least one did express a concern about the loss of control over her classroom that is part and parcel of student-centered learning. In describing to me her classroom activities pertinent to 9/11, she shared her concern

## 96  9/11 and Collective Memory in U.S. Classrooms

about opening up group discussion. Her concerns were the amount of time preparing them for a worthwhile discussion would take. Her students were not yet "mentally cooked" for such a weighty topic. As mentioned previously, the memorial of 9/11 is just after the typical beginning of most public schools, leaving scarce time for trust building, developing classroom community and providing background regarding 9/11. She also worried that an open group discussion "could lead to a ruckus". This lack of control seemingly was too uncomfortable for her to take the risk.

Another way teachers found to empower students to be the authors, and not just readers, of history is treating 9/11 as a full research unit. An important part of learning history is its collective nature; interacting with people present during a particular event, with members of other generations and with one's peers enables students to form their own views, to gain a variety of perspectives and correspondingly to possibly encounter narratives which may well differ from the official lines. Teachers 4, 3 (and others) encouraged students to ask their parents about their memories, views and opinions of 9/11 and the subsequent political and military responses. Activities such as inviting in a guest speaker, creating opportunities for students to interact with other students around the country, or collecting oral histories from older family and friends goes a long way to creating a narrative of 9/11 which is more rich and complex than might otherwise be. Given serious questions about the ability of the media to present a varied and nuanced account, the ability of schools to do so becomes even more vital. Providing students with this variety of perspectives from the community in a sense generates a "people's history of 9/11" as Howard Zinn might have it. By the nature of research or oral history itself, the standardized curriculum and even the teacher him or herself has less power to control the narrative. Again the more students can gather oral histories, dialogue and in other ways be the authors, and not mere readers, of history, the less likely it is that a hegemonic, simplistic narrative will be reproduced in the coming decades. Recalling Cobb's observation that the most violent narratives are the most simplistic ones (Cobb 2013, 100), we can now see the importance of pedagogies which open space for students to explore and question. Destabilizing violent narratives is necessary to transform a conflict.

Yet as we have seen in this chapter, teachers face significant barriers to teaching about 9/11 in a sufficiently complex and historically grounded manner. Also, teachers of course come from a variety of different political perspectives. Only rarely are teachers able to devote more than a day to 9/11. The result is that the narrative about 9/11 that students inherit is often thin, simplistic and decontextualized. Some teachers do what they can from their classroom to challenge this simplicity, but one has to question if one classroom experience can destabilize narratives absorbed in the media, at home and elsewhere. In an age of Islamophobia and centralization of standards and curriculum, the barriers are real. Chapter 5 explores the most pertinent barriers in detail.

# 5 School Culture and the Power of Neoliberalism

"I think the real barrier is internal", said Teacher 1 in response to my question regarding barriers to teaching about 9/11. And indeed, a key finding of my in-depth interviews was the subtle nature of the barriers to teaching 9/11. Again, only 30% of teachers expressed that they experienced *overt* or *explicit* barriers to doing a lesson on the events of 9/11. Given that this is the case, we need somehow to account for why it is not addressed in schools commonly, at least not in a substantive way. Remember, only a third of teachers who do teach 9/11 at all do so beyond the day of commemoration.

As teachers responding to my survey reported, there is not a notable lack of curriculum or resources. While some teachers did critique their textbooks as outdated or insufficiently in-depth, the internet age offers what most of my participating teachers found to be enough resources. A teacher who felt strongly enough that 9/11 must be taught can easily enough find what he or she needs online . Given the moving and sincere expressions of a sense of patriotic duty by the teachers I interviewed, and the availability of information, what accounts for the fact that 9/11 is more often than not, not really taught? I offer in this chapter some reasons why I think this might be.

This chapter will explore the three major barriers to teaching 9/11 that emerged from my data. One is the painful nature of the content. While teachers did not seem to report that this was a predominant barrier, it was something they had to manage for both themselves and their students. The more major barriers are finding the time to include something not necessarily in one's prescribed curriculum, and the political nature of teaching about 9/11. We have touched on these barriers throughout Ch. 3 and 4 but will explore them more in depth now.

Many layers of social, historical, political and economic context are essential for understanding what I see as the barriers that teachers encounter today. As I write, public schools face unprecedented attack from wealthy and politically conservative forces that wish to weaken unions and model public schools after the corporate world, exposing public schools to market forces, if not outrightly privatizing them. These attacks have come in the form of the increasingly centralized and standardized control as Common Core begins being implemented and high-stakes scantron testing tracks

## 98   *9/11 and Collective Memory in U.S. Classrooms*

students into their futures. As any reader following the education news will know, this is also more and more the only means of evaluating teachers. These tests determine merit pay, continuing contract (tenure), promotion and firing. Such is not a context in which especially new teachers, often full of passion and creative energy but economically very insecure and pedagogically inexperienced, are likely to innovate or take risks. The risks for teachers of providing a complex, historically grounded and nuanced narrative of 9/11 are several-fold yet related. One risk is simply taking time away from a full and again highly standardized curriculum. Those of us involved in the perennial education debates are familiar with the problems related to "teaching to the test". What my data show, especially the interviews, is that this dynamic of teaching to the test appears to be interfering with the opportunity of the first "post 9/11 generation" to fully grasp not just what happened on 9/11 but why, as well as the controversies and complexities of the U.S. response that followed the attacks of that day. A larger layer of context is the demonization not just of teachers but of public sector workers in the U.S. in general. In the neoliberal view, teachers are seen as labor, not professionals, a main reason why they are less and less trusted to write curriculum. More like proctors, they simply implement it based on data they have not helped to collect or analyze.

### "TELL OBAMA TO PUT THE QU'RAN DOWN": TEACHING 9/11 AND THE POLITICS OF ISLAMOPHOBIA

A specific kind of political barrier teachers faced is the culture of Islamophobia that has been growing, and is now in danger of becoming entrenched. 9/11 has worrisomely become a symbol of the relationship between the U.S. and the "Muslim World". While this strain of bigotry has always been present, as a result of 9/11 it has thrived and been fed by some powerful media figures and political leaders like Sarah Palin and Sean Hannity. Most recently, in the midst of the conflict over the U.S. debt ceiling and the shutdown of the U.S. government, a man speaking at a rally ostensibly against the Affordable Care Act ("Obamacare") vowed to stay until the President "put down his Qu'ran" and lamented that the U.S. "is ruled by a President who bows down to Allah and whose rules of engagement do not allow us to defend ourselves properly". (http://politicalticker.blogs. cnn.com/2013/10/13/at-tea-party-like-rally-obama-told-to-put-the-quran-down/). Five of my participating teachers, as we noted above, reported bullying of Muslim (or 'suspected' Muslim) students. As I noted in Chapter 1, numerous other examples of this sort of post 9/11 panic exist. The succession of 9/11 with the election of America's first black president, with his famously Islamic-sounding name, is proving to be a perfect storm for some Americans. The most extreme version of the narrative is that Obama himself is something of a Manchurian candidate on behalf of Al Qaeda. Parallel, and equally bigoted, narratives about Obama being a "food stamp president" were perhaps always inevitable for America's first black president. But it is difficult to imagine this sort of narrative emerging absent 9/11which casts the democratically elected president as in league with (or at least appeasing) the group that has been America's public enemy number one since 9/11/2001 absent the traumatic collective memory of the terror of that day. Such is the context in which teachers are having to try to guide students to an understanding of 9/11 and what it means. Only the foolish (or the tenured) would invite controversy. In point of fact, Teacher 5 explicitly changed his curriculum in response to peer criticism of his use of the Michael Moore documentary *Fahrenheit 9/11*. (Moore's documentaries are considered especially by conservatives to be from a partisan and leftish point of view.) Another narrative from a colleague of mine at a Florida university further illustrates. During a discussion of my research at FSU, he shared an experience of a high school teacher in his county who showed a documentary on understanding Islam during a unit on 9/11. It seems that enough angry parents called the local school board to result in the teacher's job being threatened. I am told he has not shown the documentary again (Ron, personal correspondence, Oct 12, 2013).

To reiterate from above, and to be clear, my survey results do not show that a majority of teachers feel "academically unsafe" in teaching about 9/11. Yet I stress again how important it is to go behind the numbers. While quantitatively only a minority of teachers reported openly hostile reactions to their teaching of 9/11, the extended interviews again revealed how skilled most educators are at sensing how far they can go. They know their school boards, their administrators and are members of their communities. As a colleague of mine from Penn State observed, what is the narrative about 9/11 which is being presented that allows teachers to feel safe teaching about such a divisive and dangerous topic? I have noted before that this narrative in general is quite thin and decontextualized. We have also seen numerous examples of teachers expressing their awareness that wading too far into the politics surrounding 9/11 could have consequences. Many teachers, based on my interviews, have internalized a definition of professionalism that highly values the appearance of neutrality and the detriments and punishments that can come with being biased. Professional cultures are often invisible to those of us who are a member of them and the brutal pace of middle and high school teaching today offers little time for the luxury of reflection on the true meaning of neutrality and whether that is even possible—or valuable. Political empowerment of teachers will be necessary as part of a solution to this narrowing and constriction of what ought to be (and what in the hands of some exceptional teachers is) a vital and rich curriculum.

## EMOTIONAL AND PSYCHOLOGICAL BARRIERS

One comparatively minor barrier was the strong sense of responsibility teachers felt when taking on such a subject as 9/11. Teacher 1 spoke, for

## 100   9/11 and Collective Memory in U.S. Classrooms

example, of a sense of great responsibility to teach accurate information. She also expressed a concern about taking care to not reproduce stereotypes of Muslims or Arabs. She works in her curriculum to "make sure I'm helpful with critical thinking not fueling anger" Another natural barrier for many teachers I interviewed (even when they did not let this barrier stop them) was the painful and emotional nature of the subject. "It brings up vulnerability," as one teacher expressed it. "I want to do the right thing." Teacher 11 explained that during her activities on 9/11, she once had a student become so upset that he had to leave the classroom. In a corollary observation, she noted how many of her students complained that "everything in history is something horrible". She expressed that this has, during some years, given her reason not to teach about 9/11, as she does not want to give this impression to her students. In another instance, a parent emailed her to complain about being upset by the lesson.

In addition to managing the politics and traumatized emotions of colleagues, students and parents, of course, teachers have to deal with their own emotions. At first reporting that she felt detached from the subject of 9/11 since she had not suffered a personal loss, Teacher 11 reflected as we spoke and came to conclude that this was not so. Teaching about 9/11 "is draining at the end of the day, even though I said I was removed", she observed. As one would expect with collective grief and traumatic emotions, in some respects she found teaching about 9/11 "cathartic" but on some days, having to repeat the same tragic lesson hour after hour, "I just felt on edge". She suspects that this is a primary reason that 9/11 is not taught more consistently, and in more depth, than it is.

As many peace education theorists note, we educators do not stop being parties to the conflicted history we may be teaching about (Davies 2008, Duckworth forthcoming Jan 2015). Some (8 of the 24) teachers I interviewed noted some sort of personal connection to 9/11 such as having lost or almost lost a loved one. As Teacher 5 elaborated, "Every year it is an emotional time for me. I began teaching in 2001, the images of the planes crashing into the North and South Towers replay over and over in my mind. My uncle, Col. [name redacted] at the time was employed at the Pentagon. I will always remember the calls between me and my grandmother on September 11, 2001, learning that he was not in the wing [of the Pentagon] that was hit by the third plane. Teaching about 9/11 was and will continue to be an emotional experience". For some teachers this intense emotion was a barrier to teaching about 9/11 which prevented them from doing so; for others, enduring the painful and sometimes quite personal memories was a professional and patriotic sacrifice they needed to make, as not addressing 9/11 at all was unimaginable. In fact, for some teachers, conveying and impressing the emotion upon students too young to remember 9/11 for themselves was a central goal of the lesson or unit and was seen as a means of inspiring and instilling patriotism.

Some teachers were from NYC or (like myself) Washington, DC. This connection made some teachers cautious and deeply thoughtful about the

## School Culture and the Power of Neoliberalism 101

best way to approach teaching 9/11, especially with regards to caring for the needs of any students who had been directly impacted. One teacher who had taught in NYC explained that her students "could see people jumping" from the Twin Towers. This teacher explained that "we have some kids who are highly anxious" about 9/11 and national security and so felt a professional duty to present the terrible facts without reinforcing fear and trauma. Of course this is a difficult balance to strike and teachers must rely on their abilities to know their students well enough to judge how best to proceed. Teacher 15 engaged this theme in detail. She expressed concern that, given her school's proximity to Washington, DC, she was "unsure what might come up" should a student in her classroom have experienced a personal loss on 9/11. Her experience has been that it is best not to censor the material but to warn students how intense it is. She manifested some personal hesitation as regards teaching 9/11 when I asked her why she chose to teach it. Despite this obvious emotion, she shared a near-loss with her students: "I didn't really want to go into . . . whatever . . . I told some of them a friend of mine was in the buildings [the Twin Towers] and got out". No doubt this paradoxically precipitates her commitment to teaching about 9/11, as well as representing an emotional barrier she must work to overcome.

A related emotional or psychological barrier may well be a lack of confidence in one's ability to teach the material. While not a dominant theme, nine of the twenty-four teachers I interviewed expressed concern about having the necessary background on Islam, terrorism, or other historical background such as the Cold War or specifics regarding Afghanistan. For Teacher 15 (an English teacher), as an example, this is why "we didn't really" discuss Islam or terrorism. "I am not equipped", she explained, "I don't have a lot of personal knowledge". Nor would one necessarily expect expertise on world history or terrorism from an English teacher, but recall that one of the history teachers I spoke with expressed similar concerns. This is where barriers that I have been separating for reader clarity (time, emotions) seem connected. With such increasing demands on their time and ever more standardized curriculum which they must implement (or risk censure or contract non-renewal), there is less time for teachers to develop themselves professionally in other respects. Logically this would include developing more expertise on subjects related to 9/11.

### STATE POLICY OR INSTITUTIONAL BARRIERS: THE GLASS WALL

Throughout this book I have referred to the impact of increasing standardization, bureaucratization and high-stakes testing on how teachers approach teaching 9/11. This finding came through clearly, even dominantly, in my interviews. Surely a similar dynamic effects how they approach teaching other subjects as well. A number of the teachers I spoke with were explicit, passionate and angry especially when they described the ways in which standardized tests and centralized curriculum were

## 102   *9/11 and Collective Memory in U.S. Classrooms*

disrupting their classrooms. In Teacher 19's words, " . . . the whole standards part of it is anti-teacher", though he agreed that if indeed we must reduce assessment to high-stakes scantron tests, it is probably wise to ensure teachers are on the same page. He explicitly regretted that the movement to control and centralize curriculum left so little time to engage with relevant and contemporary subjects like 9/11 in particular, and more contemporary history more related to his diverse students in general. As he noted, "If I were really going to teach about 9/11, I'd have to teach the whole history of South East Asia and I just can't. There is just no place for 9/11." For him it was much more important that the students remember, for example, his lesson on 9/11 involving the children's book *14 Cows for America* than that "they remember the five dynasties of ancient China". His state is in the middle of realigning to Common Core, and he fears this will only further aggravate the barrier of time teachers have to devote to socio-emotional, social justice and in general simply more meaningful and relevant learning. "We continue", he explains, "to get mandates regarding curriculum and testing from [state] but the result is that other necessary aspects of learning are ignored". 9/11, it seems, is not on the test. An experienced, successful (and tenured) teacher, he says he will of course comply with state standards but refuses to allow multicultural and social justice education get "short shrift" (as he puts it) and so "we're going to just make time to do it". He is aware of the challenges, even for someone who is well-liked and respected by his administration, as he reports. "It's going to be a matter of being creative and subversive— it's subversive because it's not in the Common Core." He illustrated this point with a story about a graduate student he mentors who was taking a class on teaching social justice. He was torn on how best to guide her in such a politicized and insecure environment for particularly new teachers. "There is a little side of me saying it's [social justice curriculum] not in the standards. . . . I hope she takes the message that you do it anyway". That said, he also does not want her to expose herself to administrative discipline or even being fired as a non-tenured teacher. "As soon as she gets tenure she can start being sneaky", he joked to me.

Another teacher stated, "Common [name of state] Standards are used so that is the guide that teachers have to teach by so, many teachers say that there isn't room to teach about 9/11. The curriculum is tight with specific outlined course material." Teacher 2, who described her experience with her school system as "abominable", noted that schools will not attract good teachers "if you aren't going to pay them". Her internalized disempowerment was clear: "I'm not a curriculum writer and I'm not in charge". As a whole, she felt her state did not value education. Contrast this view with the call of educational philosophers like Henry Giroux for teachers to be public intellectuals—a call I suspect this teacher would welcome were she not presently so discouraged. She elaborated that the state curriculum interferes with the building of trust and community needed to address 9/11 and

## School Culture and the Power of Neoliberalism 103

similarly controversial or painful subjects. Teacher 7 was equally explicit: "We get so bogged down with standards ... are the kids going to be able to pass this or that if I don't cover it ... that's a detriment to us as educators ... we don't have much in regards to flexibility". Given the restrictive state standards he was expected to follow, he said 9/11 "is not really a part of what we teach in U.S. history, at least the 1st semester". He reminds us that "meeting standards [meaning the standardized curriculum] is part of your evaluation as a teacher". In other words, stray from the approved curriculum and one's contract, one's very employment, could be at risk.

Teacher 11 also struggled with finding time to fit 9/11 into to a standardized and centralized curriculum: "It's kind of about where I can fit it in", she tells me. In her World History class (as opposed to her American studies class), she finds herself "just mentioning it" when the curriculum comes to South East Asia. Teacher 23 expressed a nearly identical observation: "It [9/11] doesn't match up with the Common Core". Teacher 10, as with her colleagues, was clear about this. Prior to each 9/11, in her words, "a reminder goes out to be careful" about how one approaches the controversial content. One colleague of hers, in the same school, was forced to offer parents and students an apology for what was perceived to be an anti-war bias when parents apparently complained. As she reported, one parent was angered that "You're telling kids it's bad to go to war and I'm a veteran." Teacher 10 explained her view that this had lead to teachers avoiding the topic in the classroom altogether. "Other teachers," she explained, "have had really bad things—I mean not bad, but parent complaints". She herself does not even mention that her fiancé is a veteran as she does not want "want them to think I'm all for war". The formal approach to teaching 9/11 focuses on uncritical patriotism. Her school does a yearly moment of silence but that is all.

Teacher 11 told of similar concerns regarding the need to intuit as a professional where the proverbial line was that must not be crossed when teaching about 9/11. She expressed that "no one has ever tried to limit me" and indeed observed that "If you tried to eliminate controversial history, nothing would be left". At the same time, she was clearly aware of her boundaries. This is why, for example, she found it useful to have formal curriculum on 9/11 available. Having developed curriculum for her meant that "you are doing it in a way that's fair and keeps you out of trouble". What strikes me is the consistent internalized sense of boundaries—what I am calling the "glass wall". It is highly plausible, based on my data, that so many participating teachers are not experiencing overt censorship or hostility to their approach to 9/11 because they have not (with the exception of Teacher 6) broached the subject in a controversial manner. No one really needs to articulate the consequences when the culture is understood, nor is much overt enforcement necessary when consent has been manufactured. This is part and parcel of how culture functions; we are often unaware of our cultural rules until we break them.

104 *9/11 and Collective Memory in U.S. Classrooms*

Consider this observation particularly in context of the national educational trend of high-stakes testing, narrowly quantitative assessment tools for students, teachers and administrators alike. Increasingly insecure teacher contracts, lowered pay and the scapegoating of teachers as what is "wrong with" our schools also characterizes the context in which teachers today work. Teachers in the Florida county where I live have recently lost 3% of their pension, as well as all of their step increases. Michelle Rhee, formerly Chancellor of Washington, DC Public Schools, became a controversial education reform celebrity after having fired several hundred teachers in one fell swoop. The mayor and her supporters stood by her, but public outrage ensued as well. Claims by her educational administration varied as to whether the teachers were fired for incompetence or laid off to balance DC's budget. Some of the teachers were later rehired. While this certainly does not characterize every school system, it is typical of our most troubled school systems. Further it does illustrate the national political and cultural context in which teachers must operate. This is the context in which they must decide what to teach and how. How much risk is worth taking? I am struck that teachers participating in my study seem to have seen as much, if not more, risk in deviating from the standardized curriculum as they did in addressing hot-button political issues.

## TEACHING 9/11, THE STANDARDIZATION MOVEMENT AND COMPETING NOTIONS OF CITIZENSHIP

What's Michelle Rhee got to do with a book on peace building, contested narratives and teaching 9/11? I did not intend to address the "ed reform" debates in this book, never really anticipating that they would be relevant to the teaching of 9/11. But the data, especially from my in-depth interview with teachers, was undeniable. In retrospect, it ought to have been obvious that the attempts to attack the public sector via our public schools, which overlaps with the 9/11 era, would be salient. I did anticipate the relevance of political debates about how to best defend ourselves from terrorist attacks, and guessed that teachers would experience some difficulty, and even fear, in trying to navigate these political waters of academic freedom and "neutrality". But I did not foresee how often the reduction of so much of contemporary middle and high school education to high-stakes, standardized testing would be reported by teachers as impeding their ability to teach about 9/11 as fully and comprehensively as they would like.

In this section, I contend that these barriers to teaching 9/11 constitute dangerous barriers to citizenship education itself. Developing caring, creative, critically-minded and productive citizens has been, of course, a primary goal of American education since Horace Mann. What we have is schools at the center of the storm between two competing visions for what

## School Culture and the Power of Neoliberalism    105

citizenship in a capitalist democracy ought to be. Neoliberal reformers, attacking the private sector worldwide as bloated, corrupt and ineffective, seek ways to privatize numerous sectors of democratic, public institutions, such as education, health care and national security. For this book I researched both the privatization of the security and military sector (see Priest and Arkin 2011 or Maddow 2012) and quickly realized it was necessary to further research the increasing privatization of our schools as well, particularly through neoliberal policy proposals such as vouchers, parent triggers and certain charter schools (see Ravitch 2013 for the best and newest analysis of this on the market). The nexus of this research on two different sectors not often considered together was fascinating to me, as it clarified the ideological contest currently underway regarding what citizenship ought to mean, who determines this and what the proper role of the government in a democracy is. Fundamental to what I am calling the "9/11 era" is the question of liberty and security. Schools, at least from high school on, and perhaps middle school in developmentally appropriate ways, must be spaces where students can be challenged to consider those questions. The more our schools are effectively (if not overtly) privatized, and placed into the control of Wall St. hedge fund managers (Ravitch 2013, pp. 206–223–), the less intellectual freedom and career protections a teacher will have. Concurrent with this de-facto privatization is a toxic political atmosphere that demoralizes and demonizes especially public school teachers. Education has long been the only profession thought of as though only minimal preparation and training is necessary, barely a profession at all. Yet what we see today is new. The neoliberal view of citizenship, visible currently in both the security/surveillance sector and public education, sees full citizenship as worthy only of those it defines as "makers", not to be extended to takers. Teachers, at least public school teachers especially in minority districts, are considered takers in this view, part of the "47%" if you will. They do not produce results, the argument goes, and hide behind unions to protect their lazy and incompetent workforce.

Just as millions have been made off of the private industry around surveillance and security post 9/11 (Priest and Arkin 2011), millions are being made by for-profit corporations given charters to run schools who often do not perform as well as, or about the same as, the local public schools from which they have diverted funds (Ravitch 2013, pg. 18–19). One view, the neoliberal view, of citizenship, disregards any sort of collective efforts or protection of the public commons. One's worth as a citizen can be measured by the profits one makes. This is opposed to the view of citizenship which the teachers in my study most seemed to value, connected with notions of patriotism, service, democratic decision-making processes and shared responsibility for the public commons (which include both defense and education). Nor are the two trends in these

106    *9/11 and Collective Memory in U.S. Classrooms*

sectors unconnected. They both have stemmed from nationalist fears of losing strength, security and relevance in a changing, post 9–11 (some would even say post-American) world.

How do we teach citizenship, let alone peace, in such times? The idea of the "hidden curriculum" has long been a part of educational theory and is worth revisiting here. This theory states that the socialization and hidden assumptions, most importantly what is NOT taught, of the curriculum are as impactful in shaping students as workers and citizens as anything a teacher explicitly teaches. Critical pedagogues have long discussed the hidden curriculum as a means of dampening dissent (Apple, 1971; Malott and Porfilio 2011). In her recent unveiling of the privatization efforts underlying the educational reform movements, Ravitch (2013) puts it well, arguing as I do that we cannot possibly educate students to become participants in a democracy when schools themselves are not run democratically. She writes, "No reform effort is so urgent and necessary that it requires the suspension of democracy" (p. 288). Much educational theory, but also plain common sense, tells most of us that experience is the best teacher. In an era where parent triggers and for-profit charters can suspend or overrule elected school boards, where teachers and principals have lost control of their schools, or on an even larger scale, where the entire city of Detroit can be run by an appointed "emergency manager", what can today's students possibly be internalizing about human conflict resolution processes, citizenship and democracy?

As I say, I did not plan to address the "school wars" in this book. Yet the more I listened to teachers, the more they were clearly telling me that their context of precarious employment, and even more so the loss of ability to create and implement a curriculum relevant and meaningful for their students due to a hollowed-out and scantron dictated curriculum, impedes their ability to help students understand and grapple with the challenges of the post-9/11 era.

I am lead to then ask two questions.

1. Can today's young people understand the world today without a sufficient understanding of the events of 9/11 and the era that day has shaped?
2. Given the above teacher narratives, it is reasonable to expect teachers as a whole to teach about one of the most divisive, painful and significant events in U.S. history?

My interview data in particular suggests that doing so is risky, especially if a teacher wishes to bring into the discussion various "fallout" issues such as Guantanamo Bay, water-boarding, surveillance and the occupations of Iraq and Afghanistan or the role of the U.S. in the world. This becomes even more true if a teacher wishes to examine the "causes" of 9/11, which risks challenging the founding myth of essential American innocence through which 9/11 is viewed. It has been my thesis that for sustainable peace building between the U.S. (and allies) and "the Muslim World", the narrow and extremist narratives on both sides of the conflict must be addressed. Next we recall the powerful role of schools in shaping our national and political identities. Is critical peace education possible in U.S. public schools today? And if not, can we comprehensively transform this conflict absent curriculum? Where to from here? To these questions we turn in the final chapter.

# 6 Teaching 9/11 as an Opportunity for Narrative Conflict Transformation

Narrative work in conflict resolution, at least in some sense, has been a part of the field for some time now (Cobb 2013, Winslade and Monk, 2008). Yet as conflict resolution scholars and practitioners continue to work towards designing means of sustainably building peace and transforming conflicts at their root, the "narrative turn" in the field has continued to grow. As peace educators have been saying for several decades now, classrooms are an ideal and necessary space for this narrative and collective identity work. To guide the work of classroom teachers along these lines, then, this chapter will draw on the data explored above to identify key lessons for teachers wishing to engage students in the peace and social justice work of deconstructing violent narratives (which of course serve to justify manifest violence) and constructing with others in the classroom new narratives which open space for a more peaceful future.

A few points about the dynamics and behavior of extremist narratives, a key driver of intractable conflicts, are of use here. One such insight, essential to peacebuilding and human rights, was perhaps best articulated by the 20th-century political philosopher Hannah Arendt (2009). Seyla Benhabib, following Arendt, offered a similar view (2011). To narrate, to articulate one's own story, is part and parcel of being human in this approach to human rights. To speak is to have agency. Without the actualized (as opposed to merely theoretical) ability to participate in the intersubjective, communicative processes (see Habermas 1981) of society and democracy, one remains an object rather than a subject of society. This sort of inequality we know to be a common driver of conflict throughout history. It goes without saying that teachers cannot transform this sort of cultural and historical violence alone, but as I argued throughout Chapter 2, schools are key shapers of our personal and social identity. The positioning of particular social groups, the framing of certain events in history, the erasing of other events, and the unpacked or unexamined cultural assumptions about human nature, history and the nature of knowledge itself are all relevant here. Nor is narrative conflict resolution work in schools a substitute for

*Teaching 9/11 as an Opportunity* 109

policy and institutional transformation where needed. Yet for the sake of clarity, the ways in which classrooms can implement narrative conflict resolution as one means of intervention is our focus here. I would argue these two techniques are in fact related to each other; narrative transformation is a part of what begins to make policy and institutional change on a larger social and political scale seem desirable or even possible.

Narrative conflict resolution theory tells us that the more simple and "closed" a narrative, the more likely that narrative is to lend itself to manifest (by which I mean actual, physical) violence (Cobb 2013). A narrative is closed when it precludes possibilities for any other alternative ways of being, behaving or relating to the Other, oneself and the world. In the specific case of a political leader or political party calling for war, the enemy is positioned as an existential threat. Complicating and opening up this narrative in as democratic and organic a means as possible is necessary for the narrative transformation that will enable peace building. What this means for teachers facilitating dialogues on history, literature, culture, current events and similar is that designing experiences where students can be exposed to, engage with and contest, many different historical narratives is vital.

Throughout Chapter 1 we examined the nature of 9/11 as a chosen trauma. Linking this argument to what we know from above about closed or extremist narratives, a way forward becomes clearer. Students must have the opportunity to create their own meaning around this event. They must be able to hear a variety of perspectives about the events of 9/11 and meaningfully participate in dialogues about why it occurred, what this means for Americans (and the world) and how best to seek justice, healing and a more peaceful future. They must be welcome in a democratic dialogue in which they co-create their own definition of justice. In the age of cheap-to-free global communications, fostering international dialogues between classes can be readily possible (where schools have the needed technology). Students need opportunities to explore their own definitions of concepts like justice, peace, liberty and patriotism in the context of the post-9/11 world. The essence of peace education, as I have argued in other writings (Duckworth 2011, Duckworth in Duckworth and Kelley 2012), is designing multi-disciplinary, community-based learning experiences through which students can partner with diverse others to collaboratively address problems which confront the community. The key problem we have all faced, as an American community and a global community, is how best to achieve security without compromising liberty. I contend that these sorts of CPE experiences, if skillfully designed and implemented, can provide the space and opportunity for destabilizing extremist narratives that have taken hold on both sides of the conflict between the U.S. and "the Islamic World".

What is narrative destabilization and why does it matter for sustainable conflict resolution? Macro historical narratives take hold through some concrete and identifiable processes and mechanisms—such as government

110    *9/11 and Collective Memory in U.S. Classrooms*

bodies and initiatives (like Ministries of Culture, public museums or the naming of memorials, parks and streets), media, family, faith communities and of course schools. In more extreme circumstances, governments make overt efforts to erase violent or guilt-ridden aspects of history (Barkan 2000). As extremist narratives emerge, take shape, gain power and metastasize, they preclude the possibility of counter-narratives. They do this by positioning the narrative, and probably the speakers as well, as illegitimate and immoral. In some cases the silencing is direct and overt, as in the 1994 genocide in Rwanda, but in other cases it may be more subtle. What is necessary then for teachers to do is destabilize, confront and speak back to the hegemonic narrative and empower students to participate in the public co-creation of a new narrative. Schools are in need of community partners to accomplish this, a point to which I will return shortly.

The narrative on both "sides" in the wider conflict between the U.S. and the "Islamic World" is perilously closed and extreme. That is to say, the view of the Other is thin as opposed to being able to see the Other in full human moral complexity. Further, these narratives are one-directional and contain no irony, in the sense that they do not (yet) allow for any examination of how the behavior of one's own identity group may have contributed to the conflict. Another feature of extremist narratives is that they tend to presume ill motives and a lack of integrity. This is part of how the Other is delegitimized in an extremist narrative, and thus repositioned as someone who does not have any natality, no 'right to have rights' as Arendt would phrase it. Why would a people who obviously cannot be trusted deserve a seat at the table? From here full dehumanization is a natural trajectory.

What kind of narrative then is being given to students in U.S. classrooms? Given how infrequently it is taught, and the short amount of time typically dedicated to teaching 9/11, it is hard to see how the narrative students receive can consistently from classroom to classroom be as nuanced or historically grounded as we need. Chapter Four provided fascinating and I think instructive exceptions to the rule but this must become the norm if schools are to be able to build cultures of peace in their community.

That said, where English, history and government teachers in particular are managing to carve out space in a standardized and regimented day offer much from which to build. To reemphasize a key finding of the in-depth interviews from Chapter Four, some of these teachers engage students in activities that empower students to participate in dialogic, reflective moral processes. This is so important to narrative peace building processes! For one, such activities empower young people as moral agents. This alone, I would argue, can be a beginning of destabilizing a violent or extremist narrative. Secondly, some educators invited students to research on their own, gather narratives of 9/11 from friends and family, write their own 9/11 narratives when students were old enough to recall, and debate urgent issues still facing us of liberty, security, peace and justice. When this does occur, students become agents and authors of history, not just history's objects

*Teaching 9/11 as an Opportunity*    111

or students. This furthers the "destabilizing" of the hegemonic narrative around 9/11 as such narratives find much more difficulty taking root in democratic, communicative contexts where equal subjects together shape and make meaning around collective history. Educational philosophers from John Dewey to Maria Montessori and Howard Zinn of course have spoken on the importance of this type of agency for advancing social justice and building democratic citizenship, which are of course important aspects of a culture of peace.

Still, even more can and should be done. Wherever possible, especially non-Muslim students need to hear from their Muslim peers who are of course the Other in the context of this conflict. This may or may not happen organically through facilitating class-to-class dialogues online depending on the demographics of the school. We also saw in Chapter 4 examples of some teachers directly engaging stereotypes of Muslims and Islam, typically through class discussion or documentaries but sometimes also through guest speakers or though making skillful pedagogical use of the diversity of the classroom. Teachers also spoke of ways in which they directly challenged, contradicted and corrected uneducated statements or views of Islam. Recall from Ch 4. that many teachers I interviewed found it necessary to directly counter harmful cultural narratives about Muslims which have long been present but which have become increasingly salient, extreme and entrenched since 9/11. I am mindful here too of the five teachers who reported concern about bullying of Muslim students. Not one of these teachers felt their school had done enough to protect these students or resolve the incidents that had occurred. Further, it is likely that this particular kind of bullying is under-observed and under-reported, as Muslim students will often not wear traditional dress or openly identify themselves as Muslim precisely for fear of bullying. Perhaps this is one reason that teachers themselves are not always aware of Muslim students in the class. Teacher 15 noted this explicitly, stating that there are "probably Muslim students at [her] school but [she's] not sure". Classrooms and schools that are aspiring to a culture of peace will do their best to prioritize bringing marginalized voices to the fore. This has to mean teachers, parents and administrators insisting that the time and space in a classroom needed to build community be protected, not crowded out by testing.

Another narrative I believe that needs deconstructing, and then improving, is the professional narrative of teacher neutrality. This narrative seems to be functioning for teachers in a similar way as it does for journalists. In both cases, neutrality serves the status quo. As someone who myself taught for seven years in our public schools, I find it so easy to empathize with teachers who express this professional value and in some ways I share it myself as a teacher now before a graduate classroom teaching peace education and international conflict resolution. I sometimes withhold my own view of a particular issue or debate so as not to sway students or phrase myself in a much more careful manner than I would outside the classroom.

## 112   9/11 and Collective Memory in U.S. Classrooms

At the same time, what and who does this culture of ostensible neutrality, this narrative, really serve? Where do we reach the tipping point from a teacher not "indoctrinating" her students to promoting a sense of false equivalence between arguments that are not equal? When does substance become sacrificed to neutrality? This culture of neutrality itself can perhaps explain why so many teachers did not necessarily perceive overt barriers (in the sense of censorship or articulated administrative or parental concern) between them and their teaching of 9/11. There is little need to censor journalists who do not attempt to fundamentally challenge political leaders. Similarly there is little need to censor or discipline teachers or curriculum writers who do not fundamentally challenge the status quo of our schools today. If the narrative of 9/11 presented is thin or exclusively orthodox, or does not deviate from the sanctioned, official narrative, the barriers that, at least to my mind, clearly exist could well remain invisible. Typically we as humans are not aware of cultural barriers until we have disregarded them. Are we seeing here a manifestation of the manufacture of consent, as Gramsci or Chomsky might argue (Simon 1991, Chomsky and Herman, 2002)? Narrative conflict resolution focuses considerably on the need for people as moral agents to articulate themselves and their views. No one is arguing that teachers ought to tell students "what to think" but neither can we present all sides of an argument as equally right or just. This would be the history curriculum equivalent of defending any cultural practice, regardless of its violation of human rights.

I have been arguing that in many ways, the barriers to going beyond the official narrative regarding 9/11 may be internalized by teachers, as we can see in the professional culture of neutrality that cannot truly be achieved and in some ways is not even desirable. Yet in some cases, clearly teachers experienced and articulated them overtly. The need some teachers expressed to avoid the controversial issues is also a real concern with respect to the narrative students are inheriting about the meaning of 9/11. Teachers (and their students) deserve an educational environment in which they feel they can question orthodoxies, make meaning and address controversies without fear of reprisal. While only a few teachers explicitly felt that there would be consequences as measured in my quantitative data, the subtle self-censoring of some teachers was clear from the qualitative interviews I conducted. In effect, the results in the classroom are the same: a narrative about 9/11 that is thin, ahistorical and decontextualized. This prevents the narrative transformation needed for sustainable conflict resolution.

As Foucault (1982) so seminally theorized, to construct knowledge is to hold power. If students do not experience learning contexts that allow them to question power, they can hardly help but absorb and reproduce the narratives already dominant. In the case of 9/11, of course, we are discussing a narrative of innocent victimhood and trauma that justified revenge, as well as restrictions on civil liberties. The dynamics of chosen trauma suggest that this narrative will continue to be destructively reproduced unless the generations "post 9/11" are helped to write a more historical, empathic, complex and ironic story.

A narrative component of 9/11 that does not appear addressed by my participants is one of the U.S. founding myths, a cornerstone of what is often called our "civil religion". I refer here to American Exceptionalism. As I suggested in Chapter One, this myth has shaped the collective narrative of 9/11 that is emerging, as it has shaped our understanding of most other major events in U.S. history. Yet only a few teachers I spoke with explicitly engage students in activities and dialogues that invite them to challenge this narrative. Perhaps a student will then go on to reject or continue questioning the narrative, perhaps not, but if the opportunity is never raised, the students' intellectual and moral space remains narrowed.

Other policy implications go beyond the classroom and remain largely outside of a teacher's control but are still worth articulating. The states that have not must immediately pass legislation requiring that the events of 9/11 be taught. Community planners and school leaders must do much more to integrate schools; integration remains a fact far more on paper than in reality even today. Schools must become a space where teachers and students alike daily encounter people from many different backgrounds. They must also become what I call "multi-track", that is, far more integrated into their communities than is presently the case. Such community partnerships can provide the resources and relationships needed to implement experiential, projected based learning. This methodology is the most conducive to narrative peace building in the classroom.

### TELLING A BETTER STORY ABOUT 9/11: NARRATIVE CONFLICT RESOLUTION

To foster narrative conflict transformation, we must not only deconstruct extremist narratives. We must replace the old, narrow, rigid narrative with what Cobb (2013, 203–227) refers to as a "better formed story". What then would a "better-formed story" about 9/11 be and how can educators help students to be a part of writing and telling it?

Narrative conflict resolution suggests that a "better formed story" about 9/11 would entail two key elements: complexity and irony. This harmonizes well with pedagogical goals of critical thinking. The most common dynamic of conflict at all levels is the tendency of the narrative of the parties to the conflict to be narrow, monodimensional and justificatory. The story of 9/11, of the suffering of Afghan civilians under Soviet occupation, or the Taliban, or resulting from the U.S.-led invasion, or the devastation of communities in Iraq after the U.S. and its "coalition of the willing" invaded it, all constitute conflict narratives. They tell the story of one's suffering, why it was undeserved, and provide justification for the party's response to said suffering or victimization. They engage mechanisms, processes and

## 114    *9/11 and Collective Memory in U.S. Classrooms*

institutions such as family, schooling, the media, faith institutions and government-sponsored narratives found at sites like memorials or museums. Needless to say, they are full of rage and pain and often seek to position the group as blameless, righteous, honest, civilized and so on. As a corollary, these narratives position "the Other" as untrustworthy, lazy, aggressive, uncivilized and even at times demonic. I noted some of this in Chapters 1 and 2, but here now with the perspective of teacher experiences in the classroom teaching 9/11, I will draw this book to a close offering some ways I think classrooms might be a part of a more comprehensive peace-building process between "the West" and "the Muslim World".

It was a pleasure and a reason for hope, I think, that we can observe some excellent practices already in today's middle and high school classrooms—and this despite considerable curricular, resource, emotional and political barriers. Two activities come to mind as reasonably replicable in today's classroom, with all of its many challenges, indeed under attack in many ways (Ravitch 2013). My aim here is to suggest activities and approaches that might help address the central problem as I see it, which is the hesitancy to address in a comprehensive and critical manner some of the more taboo topics related to 9/11, such as the role of the U.S. in the world, which critics see as imperial. This hesitancy is understandable given the climate for teachers I have been describing above, yet I will offer thoughts here on how a teacher who wishes to bring such topics into her classroom might do so without risking her job. The pressing need to change this climate as a policy matter is urgent but outside the scope of this particular work.

One such practice is engaging students in gathering and sharing oral histories about 9/11. This we could see in, for example, assignments that asked students to interview family members and report back to class. As I argued in Chapter 4, such activities can help students view themselves as agents in and authors of history, rather than history's subjects. Caution is due here, however. This result is not automatic simply because students are asked to interview folks at home; they must then be asked to reflect upon, make meaning from and critically engage with these oral histories. A powerful as an older brother or mother's memories on 9/11 are, they must be placed in historical and socio-political context for students to be able to learn from them. The teachers I spoke with consistently expressed concerns about the time they had in the curriculum to devote. This creates a considerable challenge for any teacher trying to spend long enough teaching about 9/11 to provide students with needed relevant information, like the Cold War, the Soviet invasion of Afghanistan, dynamics of U.S. foreign policy, and similar. Yet this is essential if the parties in the story here are going to become complex enough for a "better formed story" to have a chance to emerge. Part of narrative conflict resolution is about impacting power dynamics implicated in almost any human relationship. Power, as Cobb notes, "is . . . a discursive practice" (2013, 150). Dialogues and narrative work meant to intervene in a conflict then must do more than help parties understand one

*Teaching 9/11 as an Opportunity*     115

another better, or achieve a sense of empathy or responsibility. Narrative conflict resolution ultimately must help reestablish the moral legitimacy of the victim. Cobb observes similarly: "Power is a function of the way persons are positioned as moral agents" (2013, p. 161). This means more than just speaking, it means being heard. The trick here, of course, is that parties tend to vie for victim status. Here is where teachers can usefully complicate student readings of history. Which party is more powerful? How do we know this? Can someone (or some group) be both a victim and a perpetrator? What do we do when there is clearly a "more guilty party" even if wrongs have been done on all sides? In terms of teaching 9/11 then, the narrative students receive about 9/11 must work to (re)establish the moral legitimacy of Muslim speakers. As we saw in our teacher narratives, some teachers are working to do just this. Yet I would again caution us against any expectation that schools alone can accomplish such tremendous work. Media, families, political regimes, economic relations and other human systems are also a part of the peace building process; it is only for the sake of clarity of focus here that I treat the role of schools.

The stories we tell about ourselves, our history and the history of the Others shape, and in some key ways, limit our moral imagination. As Hughes noted (2003), American civic religion is founded on the interconnected myths of the U.S. being both a Chosen nation, chosen by God to be a representative of His Kingdom on Earth, as well America being a wholly Christian nation. Our cultural narratives, without reifying them, can set boundaries of the possibilities we are able to perceive. So a second classroom practice that can serve as a means of disrupting and replacing harmful conflict narratives is the use of material that challenges student stereotypes of Islam and Muslims. This of course will involve teachers helping students to explicitly examine and, where appropriate, deconstruct the above referenced myths. We saw this most clearly when we heard from teachers who chose documentaries that would challenge student preconceived narratives of who Muslims are (such as "Faith, Fasting and Football") or other documentaries which similarly presented Muslims in three dimensions, humanizing the Other. Recall one teacher's documentary selection specifically noted the impact of 9/11 on Muslims and showed the outrage of most Muslims regarding 9/11. Other teachers invited in guest speakers, in particular local leaders from the Muslim and other faith communities, to provide students with some beginning of Thich Nhat Hahn's "direct encounter". While this is not occurring with nearly the frequency we need for schools to be successfully destabilizing dominant narratives about Islam, we do have such classroom practices to build upon. As a policy matter, the defacto segregation of our schools remains an impediment. Again, building on the notion of the importance of a "direct encounter" for peacebuilding (reasonably similar to the contact hypothesis), students and teachers cannot have this opportunity in communities that are not racially, ethnically and religiously diverse. Today's risk-adverse, creatively stifled and testing-driven

# 116 *9/11 and Collective Memory in U.S. Classrooms*

approach to education views taking the time to honor and educate about various cultures in the school community as a distraction and a risk. This could not be further from the truth; it is relevant and valuable content than can empower schools, with their communities, to address the conflicts that face them and prepare future leaders.

A third, and I think most powerful, "best practice" was not commonly seen in my data. This would be to incorporate the teaching of 9/11 into an overall thematic unit focused on causes of violence, stereotypes, the need for intercultural understanding and the dangers of scapegoating. In turn such units must be taught throughout the year and incorporated into building and system-wide actions to build a school culture of peace. Much has been written on the theory behind this and practices schools can put into place (Duckworth, Williams and Allen, 2011; Duckworth 2011; Duckworth in Duckworth and Kelley 2012; Bajaj 2006; Lantieri and Patti 1996; Freire 2003; Montessori 1949/1972; Beckerman and Zembylas 2012). Briefly here, the key point is that while creative and courageous individual teachers can make a tremendous difference in the worldviews of their students, isolated instances of a critical historical dialogue are not likely to be sufficient. School and community leaders must partner to engage students and teachers in dialogues and collaborative problem solving based in an interdisciplinary curriculum. Media and faith leaders would be especially appropriate partners in the case of dialogues around 9/11 collective narratives. The mantra of peace education? Problems make the best curriculum. If the problem at hand is peace and security, specifically relevant to relations between Christians, Muslims and Jews, and between the West and the Muslim world, the curriculum development "essential question" becomes what to do about this? Units involving math, science, history, research, presentation and writing can be developed around such questions vital to our democracy as

1. What is in fact the wisest balance between liberty and security? How have societies addressed this question throughout history?
2. How have peoples in history handled fear, loss and trauma? What lessons can we draw?
3. Is religion a "cause" of conflict and if so, why (or why not)?
4. What has the impact of the U.S. role in the world been throughout the 20th century? What should it be going forward? Has it fostered peace? Conflict?
5. What does in fact cause violence? How can we prevent it?
6. What do peace and justice look like in a society anyway? Have any societies achieved them? How?

To those who would argue that there is no time for such interdisciplinary, project-based learning, I would pose this question: do we or do we not in the future need leaders who can address the above? If so, then our

# Teaching 9/11 as an Opportunity 117

students need such curriculum. I direct this not at classroom teachers who must in many cases simply implement the curriculum they have been given, but rather at the policy makers who are driving "reforms" that increase rote memorization, high-stakes testing and centralized, often irrelevant standards. We must take care to note the barrier of "time" as cited by my participating teachers is a *political* barrier. The decision to divert the resource of classroom time to ancient, rather than more contemporary, history, or for example, to prioritize testing above all else, is very much a political choice based on a particular neoliberal view of what citizenship is (being a worker) and what schools ought to be about (producing workers). No one disputes that students need jobs, but the solution for that is economic policy geared for job growth (e.g. investment in R&D, infrastructure, and reversing our present course of austerity), not reducing teachers to proctors and students to one data point based on the day they took a scantron test.

Questions such as the above can help students to develop what I would call, drawing from Cobb's narrative conflict resolution theory (2013) "ironic history". Zinn might phrase this as critical history, or history from the perspective of the Other/Enemy. From the perspective of the other, the cause of the conflict at hand is U.S. imperial behavior. We've approached quite dangerous territory for teachers here. Recently I was reading about a professor in MN who was formally reprimanded by her university's Dean of Academic Affairs for teaching a lesson on structural racism. The professor's positionality as an African American woman is relevant. She introduced the theory of white privilege and three white male students filed a formal grievance for discrimination, complaining that this lesson made them uncomfortable (Cottom online). (One suspects it ought to.)

If curriculum is going to be able to incorporate narrative conflict resolution work, the stories students learn about themselves, their societies and the Other must become ironic (Cobb 2013, pp. 248–274). That is, students must have questions posed to them that aid them in seeing the complex, systemic and historical causes of a contemporary manifestation of a conflict. (Recall my observation that 9/11 was not simply a day on which attacks occurred, but an era.) Even more specifically, Cobb writes that developing a more ironic story entails the parties to a conflict becoming able to see the contributions of their own behavior to the conflict (hence the sense of irony). This would mean, in the case of my own research, asking U.S. students to see 9/11 from the viewpoint of the Other and vise versa. As I say, dangerous territory, leading us to ask the question of whether our own behavior in the world in any way contributed to 9/11, due to the U.S. imperial role in the world, and yet ultimately we must find a way to have this dialogue or remain entrapped in a cycle of violence and revenge. Many, including some teachers themselves, will feel this excuses and justifies the actions of the perpetrators of the 9/11 attacks. This cannot be the case, since nothing can justify the mass murder committed by the 19 perpetrators who crashed commercial airlines into the Pentagon, and the Twin

118  *9/11 and Collective Memory in U.S. Classrooms*

Towers. Yet events in any conflict always have a context. The unwise and punitive aspects of the Treaty of Versailles, centuries of anti-Semitism and economic depression help at least in part to explain the rise of Hitler and the atrocities of the Holocaust. They cannot ever justify it. Any dialogues around 9/11, I think, will be aided by bearing this challenging and emotional distinction in mind.

Teachers wishing to bring discussions about imperialism into their classroom can take a comparative approach, drawing off of material already in many history curricula. For example, what features did the Chinese, Soviet and British empires have in common? Does the U.S. play a similar role in the world? If yes, how so and what is the impact on other countries? If not, why so? Students can be invited to research, debate about and present on such topics, either at the classroom or even the building-wide level. Teachers will face daunting, sometimes even prohibitive, barriers to implementing such curriculum. As we are familiar with by now, the primary barriers include prescribed state curriculum, over-emphasis on standardized testing and the political controversies of the topics. It is the responsibility of school leaders, in my view, to foster a climate where such meaningful debates can be had, though I do understand at the same that school boards and administrators themselves face similar barriers. Parents, teachers and community leaders concerned that such debates indeed be realized in our schools must organize and engage state legislatures and local media to insist on a more nurturing and academically free school culture.

Americans perhaps have a unique relationship with history. We have a habit of seeing ourselves as separate from it, or at least not quite as subject to its vagaries and cruelties as other societies have been. Henry Ford, that American icon of the future, of progress and modernity, captured this when he said, "History is more or less bunk. It's tradition. We don't want tradition, we want to live in the present, and the only history that is worth a tinker's damn is the history we make today". Americans innovate and invent naturally as a cultural habit; historical reflection is not a cultural habit of ours. In a real sense, we feel that we have escaped history. Hughes (2003) refers to this as the myth of "Nature's Nation", related to the myth of America being the Chosen Nation, that city on a hill. The myth of "nature's nation" suggested that America was a blank slate, upon which any future at all could be written. This was possible because of the unique way in which this myth believes that God favors the U.S. "In other words," writes Hughes (2003), "the American system was not spun out of someone's imagination or contrived by human wit. Instead, it was based on a natural order, built into the world by God himself" (p. 56). While this arguably encourages American optimism, we cannot escape that it is a view that positions the peoples and cultures who were here before the European colonists as invisible; Manifest Destiny has been often cited as an example of this. "At its core," Hughes writes, "this myth encouraged Americans to ignore the power of history and tradition as forces that shaped the nation" (p. 56). Blessed and appointed by God, and without the history that brings "original sin", there was little need to be burdened with the past. When it comes to understanding and learning from the past, and healing collective trauma, the grappling with history that is called for goes against our cultural grain. Unlearning, then, as much as learning, is needed for narrative conflict resolution related to 9/11. Teachers helping students to grasp 9/11 and the era it defines would do well to address this directly, coaxing students to deconstruct this myth and develop an awareness of the forces and cultural myths which do indeed shape us, despite our tendency to think ourselves exceptional in comparison to other nations in this regard. I believe the rending of this myth is another reason for the deep trauma and terror of 9/11—we were invaded by history. We could no longer believe ourselves to be immune—to be exceptional. Soluka concurred elsewhere with this observation when he wrote that 9/11 was not "just a terrorist attack. This was an act of metaphysical trespass" (Hughes, 2003, p. 158). The better students understand the founding civic and cultural myths through which we understand 9/11, the better prepared they will be for the post-9/11 era.

The story about 9/11 passed down to students, at least as revealed in my data, which is only one study and needs replication for increased credibility, is most often quite thin because we the adults have not yet come to terms ourselves with the shock and terror of that day and have not yet even begun to build consensus on how best to respond. We grieve annually, we grow the security and surveillance state, tolerate as a society NYPD infiltration of mosques in Manhattan and normalize drone warfare, but this has not brought healing.

During a presentation of this research, one of our doctoral students insightfully noted to me that this book is perhaps too early. Significant, traumatic events like the mass violence of 9/11, and the era of surveillance, torture and war that followed, are processed I suspect in generations, not years. But the time is now to begin a conversation, and to develop understanding of how the first "post 9/11" generation may be processing that collective trauma. The implications of the thin, decontextualized and ahistorical narrative that too many students are receiving are worrisome, in that they do not bode well for any possibilities of narrative conflict resolution and suggest the reproduction of many of the dominant narratives that helped to drive the larger conflict between the U.S. (and allies) and the "Muslim World" to begin with. That said, there are ways forward, as I hope to have shown in the examples of those teachers I had the fortune to interview, who have found a way to bring complexity, critical thinking, deep historical analysis and perhaps even what Zembylas might call "critical emotional praxis" to their classrooms. They labor against powerful forces that have actively sought to weaken the autonomy and economic security of teachers in the classroom, and against a larger context of neoliberalism and continued Islamaphobia. Their work must succeed and be built upon if any sort of sustainable peace is to be built as we continue to process "the mourning after".

# Appendix A
## Quantitative Survey

**1. What activities have you led to teach about 9/11? Please check the appropriate box and/or write in an activity you have implemented.**

☐ group discussion

☐ guest speaker

☐ school assembly

☐ film/documentary on 9/11

☐ class research project

☐ I have not really taught about 9/11

Other (please specify)

**2. If you have not taught about 9/11, please check the box that best explains why you have not addressed 9/11 in your classroom.**

☐ a. It's not really a part of my curriculum.

☐ b. I'm not confident enough in my own knowledge.

☐ c. I don't have the time with everything else I'm expected to cover.

☐ d. I don't have the resources I need.

☐ e. It's too political.

☐ f. It's too emotional.

☐ g. Other aspects of the curriculum are more important.

Other (please specify)

**3. Many organizations have developed curriculum for teachers on the events of 9/11 (such as PBS, the Fordham Foundation and the Sept. 11 Education Project). Have you used any such curriculum? If "yes" please specify in the text box.**

☐ Yes

☐ No

Other (please specify)

## 122  Appendix A

**4. How often would you say you address 9/11?**

☐ Once a month

☐ Once a quarter

☐ Once a semester

☐ Once a year

Other (please specify)

**5. How would you characterize your students' knowledge about 9/11?**

☐ Excellent

☐ Very good

☐ Good

☐ Fair

☐ Poor

Other (please specify)

**6. Did you receive any administrative, student or parent reactions you would describe as concerned or even hostile in regard to 9/11 events or related activities? If so, please describe in the text box.**

☐ Yes

☐ No

Other (please specify)

**7. How easy is it to get the resources you need to teach about 9/11 at your school? Feel free to provide details in the text box.**

☐ extremely easy

☐ very easy

☐ moderately easy

☐ a bit difficult

☐ extremely difficult

Other (please specify)

*Appendix A*   123

**8. How free academically do you feel teaching about 9/11 at this school? Feel free to provide details in the text box.**

☐ Extremely safe

☐ Very safe

☐ Moderately safe

☐ Slightly safe

☐ Not at all safe

Other (please specify)

**9. Have you attempted to teach about 9/11 but faced barriers that resulted in not being able to (or not being able to continue a lesson/unit once you'd started)?**

☐ Parent hostile reaction

☐ Student hostile reaction

☐ Administrative hostile reaction

☐ A lack of resources/curriculum relating to 9/11

☐ A lack of time in the curriculum

☐ Too emotional or painful for me personally

☐ I do not feel I faced barriers when it comes to teaching about 9/11.

Other (please specify)

**10. We would welcome the opportunity to learn more about your experiences teaching about 9/11. Would you be willing to participate in an interview (of about an hour) in person or over the phone? (If yes, please include your phone number or email below, and we'll be happy to get in touch!)**

☐ Yes, please————my number or email is in the text box below

☐ No, thanks

Other (please specify)

# Appendix B
## 9/11 Study Interview Protocol

1. What do you teach?
2. For how long?
3. Tell us a bit about your classroom. How would you describe it?
4. What sort of activities have you done, if any, to help your student understand 9/11?
5. How did they go?
6. Would you say you have faced any political or institutional barriers to teaching 9/11?
7. Have you experienced any notably negative or positive reactions to teaching about 9/11? Tell us more.
8. If you have not directly taught about 9/11, please tell us more about why not? Has anything particular prevented this?
9. How would you describe your students' knowledge of 9/11?
10. What was it like for you teaching about 9/11? What were you thinking and feeling as you taught?

Bonus

11. We appreciate your willingness to talk to us. Anything we have not asked about that you would like to share?

# References

"39 Possible Human Remains from 9/11 Found at World Trade Center Debris". CBS Online. April 2013. Available online at http:// http://www.cbsnews.com/news/39-possible-human-remains-from-9–11-found-in-world-trade-center-debris/

Ahluwalia, Pal, et al. eds. (2012). *Reconciliation and Pedagogy*. London and New York: Routledge.

Alden, Edward. (2008). *The Closing of the American Border*. New York: Harper Perennial.

Alkana, Linda Kelly. (2011). "What Happened on 9/11: Nine Years of Polling College Undergraduates: 'It was always just a fact it happened.'" *The History Teacher* 44(4): 602—612.

Anderson, Benedict. (1991). *Imagined Communities*. Revised Ed. London: Verso.

Apple, Michael. 1971. "The Hidden Curriculum and the Nature of Conflict". *Interchange* 1(4): 27–40.

Arendt, Hannah. (2009). *The Origins of Totalitarianism*. New York: Harcourt, Brace, Jovanovich.

Azar, Edward. (1990). *The Management of Protracted Social Conflict: Theory and Cases*. Dartmouth: Aldershot.

Bacevitch, Andrew. (2013). *The New American Militarism: How Americans Are Seduced by War*. New York: Oxford.

Bajaj, Monisha, ed. (2008). *Encyclopedia of Peace Education*. Charlotte, NC: Information Age Publishers.

Bajaj, Monisha. (2012). *Schooling for Social Change: The Rise and Impact of Human Rights Education in India*. New York: Continuum Press.

Baily, Supriya. "Can you eat peace: addressing development needs and peace education in Gujarat, India." In Ndura and Amster, eds. *Building Cultures of Peace: transdisciplinary voices of hope and action*. Newcastle upon Tyne: Cambridge Scholars Publishing.

Barkan, Elazar. (2000). *The Guilt of Nations*. New York: WW Norton & Co.

Beckerman, Zvi and Zembylas, Michalinos. (2012). *Teaching Contested Narratives: Identity, Memory and Reconciliation in Peace Education and Beyond*. Cambridge: Cambridge University Press.

Benhabib, Seyla. (2011). *Dignity in Adversity: Human Rights in Troubled Times*. Malden, MA: Polity.

Berna, Dustin D. (2012). "Islamic Fundamentalism and the Egyptian Revolution." In C.L. Duckworth and C.D. Kelley (eds.) *Conflict Resolution and the Scholarship of Engagement*. Newcastle upon Tyne: Cambridge.

Bisland, Beverley Millner. (2006). "At the Edge of Danger: Elementary Teachers in Queens, New York, September 11, 2001." *Education and Urban Society* 38(4): 375–397.

## 128    References

Blight, David. (2002). *Race and Reunion: The Civil War in American Memory.* Cambridge: : Harvard University Press.

Boulding, Elise. (2000). *Cultures of Peace: the hidden side of history.* Syracuse, NY: *Syracuse Univ. Press.*

Buckner, David. (2005). *An Evaluation of Post-9/11 Arkansas Teacher Attitudes towards Civic Education.* Fayetville: University of Arkansas.

Burton, John, ed. (1990). *Conflict: Human Needs Theory.* New York: St. Martin's Press.

Cheldelin, Sandra, Daniel Druckman and Larissa Fast, eds, (2003). *Conflict.* New York, Continuum.

Chomsky, Noam. (2011). *9/11: Was There an Alternative?* New York: Seven Stories Press.

Chomsky, Noam and Edward Herman. (2002). *Manufacturing Consent.* New York: Pantheon.

Christie, Pam. (2012). "Beyond Reconciliation: reflections on South Africa's Truth and Reconciliation Commission and its implications for ethical pedagogy." in Ahluwalia, Pal, et al, eds. *Reconciliation and Pedagogy.* NY: Routledge.

Clarke, Richard. (2009) *Against All Enemies: Inside America's War on Terror.* New York: Free Press.

Cloke, Kenneth. (2008). *Conflict Revolution: Mediating Evil, War, Injustice and Terrorism.* Janis Publishers.

Cobb, Sara. (2003). "Narrative Analysis." in Cheldelin, et al, ed. Cheldelin, Druckman and Fast, eds. *Conflict,* 2$^{nd}$ ed. London: Continuum Press.

Cobb, Sara. (2013). *Speaking of Violence: The Politics and Poetics of Narrative in Conflict Resolution* Oxford, UK: Oxford University Press.

Cohen, Patricia, et al. (2006). "Current Affairs and the public psyche: American anxiety in the post 9/11 world." *Social Psychiatry and Psychiatric Epidemiology,* 2006; 41 (4):251–260.

Cole, Elizabeth, ed. (2007). *Teaching the Violent Past: History Education and Reconciliation. Lanham, MD: Rowman and Littlefield.*

Connerton, Paul. (1989). *How Societies Remember.* Cambridge, UK: Cambridge University Press.

Cottom, Tressie McMillan. "The Discomfort Zone". Online at http://www.slate. com/articles/life/counter_narrative/2013/12/minneapolis_professor_shannon_ gibney_reprimanded_for_talking_about_racism.html

Council on American Islamic Relations. "CAIR concerned by spike in anti-Muslim incidents in Ramadan." Accessed March 2014. http://www.prnewswire. com/news-releases/cair-concerned-by-spike-in-anti-muslim-incidents-in-ramadan-62137032.html

Davies, Lynn. (2004). *Education and Conflict.* London, Routledge.

Davies, Lynn. (2008). *Educating Against Extremism.* Stoke on Trent, UK: Trentham Books.

Dewey, John. *Democracy and Education.* (2008). Radford, VA: Wilder Publications.

Dewey, John. *The School and Society.* (2007). New York: Cosmio Classics. Louise Diamond and John McDonald. (1996). *Multi-Track Diplomacy: a Systems Approach to Peace.* West Hartford, CT: Kumarian Press.

Duckworth, Cheryl. (2011). *Land and Dignity in Paraguay.* New York: Continuum.

Duckworth, Cheryl, Barb Allen and Teri T. Williams. (2012). "What Do Students Learn When We Teach Peace?" *Journal of Peace Education.* 9(1): 81–99.

Duckworth, Cheryl. (2012). "The Praxis of Social Movements and Peace Education." in Duckworth and Kelley, eds. *Conflict Resolution and the Scholarship of Engagement.* New Castle upon Tyne: Cambridge.

Duckworth, Cheryl. (April 2015). "History's Hardest Questions in the Classroom: History, Memory and Peace Education." *Peace and Change.*

## References 129

Engel, Susan. (1999). *Context is Everything: the nature of memory*. NY: WH Freeman and Co.

Espiritu, Karen and Donald G. Moore. (2008). "'Beyond Ground Zero': The Futures of Critical Thought After 9/11." *The Review of Education, Pedagogy and Cultural Studies*, 30: 198–219.

Faludi, Susan. (2007) *The Terror Dream: Myth and Misogyny in an Insecure America*. New York: Picador Press.

Farenthold, David and Michelle Boorstein. "Rep Peter King's Hearings: A Key Moment in an Angry Conversation." Washington Post Online. Available online at: http://www.washingtonpost.com/wp-dyn/content/article/2011/03/09/AR2011030902061.html

Foucault, Michel. (1982). *The Archeology of Knowledge*. New York: Vintage Books.

Freire, Paulo. 2003. *Pedagogy of the Oppressed*. 30th Anniversary Ed. New York: Continuum Press.

Frommer, Frederic J. "Ellison Uses Thomas Jefferson's Quran." http://www.washingtonpost.com/wp-dyn/content/article/2007/01/05/AR2007010500512.html

Galtung, Johan. (1990). "Cultural Violence". *Journal of Peace Research*, 2(3): 291–305.

Gellner, Ernest. (2006). *Nations and Nationalism*. Oxford: Blackwell Publishers.

Giroux, Henry. (2011). "The Disappearing Intellectual in the Age of Economic Darwinism" Policy Futures in Education 9:2 (2011). pp., 163–172. Online: http://www.wwwords.co.uk/pfie/content/pdfs/9/issue9_2.asp

Goodman, David. (2012, December 11). Muslim rights group warns against anti-sharia bill. *Detroit Free Press*. Available online at: www.freep.com/article/20121211/NEWS06/121211091/Sharia-law-Michigan-legislature-Gov-Rick-Snyder-Muslim-rights-group

Goodman, Jo Victoria. "Mapping civic debate following September 11, 2001: Civic courage, social cartography and curriculum theorizing." University of Pittsburgh, 2003. 3104731.

Haas, Mary E. and Robert A. Waterson. (2011). "Dare We Not Teach 9/11 Yet Advocate Citizenship Education?" *The Social Studies*, 102(4): 147–152.

Habermas, Jurgen.(1981). *The Theory of Communicative Action*. Boston: Beacon Press.

Halbwachs, Maurice. (1992.) *On Collective Memory*. Chicago: University of Chicago Press.

Harris, Ian and Mary Lee Morrison. (2003). *Peace Education (2ⁿᵈ ed.)* Jefferson, NC: McFarland and Co.

Hart, Bary. (2008.) *Peacebuilding in Traumatized Societies*. Lanham, MD: University Press of America.

Hedges, Chris. (2002). *War Is a Force That Gives Us Meaning*. New York: Public Affairs.

Hess, Diana and Jeremy Stoddard. (2007). "9/11 and Terrorism: 'the Ultimate Teachable Moment' in Textbooks and Supplemental Curricula". *Social Education*, 71(5): 231–236.

Hess, Diana and Jeremy Stoddard. (2011). "9/11 in the Curriculum: A Retrospective." *The Social Studies*, 102(4): 175–179.

Hess, Diana and Jeremy Stoddard. "Examining the Treatment of 9/11 and Terrorism in High School Textbooks." (2008). Bixby, Janet S., and Judith L. Pace, eds. *Educating Democratic Citizens in Troubled Times: Qualitative Studies of Current Efforts*. Albany, NY: SUNY Press.

Horwitz, Sari. "ACLU asks Justice to probe surveillance of Muslims by NYPD." http://www.washingtonpost.com/world/national-security/aclu-asks-justice-dept-to-probe-surveillance-of-muslims-by-new-york-city-police-dept/2013/10/24/b667dce8-3cb4-11e3-b6a9-da62c264f40e_story.html

## 130   *References*

Hosking, Geoggery and Schöpflin, George, eds. (1997). *Myths and Nationhood.* New York: Routledge.

Hughes, Richard. (2004). *Myths America Lives By.* Urbana, IL: University of Chicago Press.

Hulette, Elisabeth. (2011). "Teaching 9/11: Attacks Prominent in History Textbooks." Hampton Roads.com. Sept. 10, 2011. Accessed online Sept. 2012 at http://hamptonroads.com/2011/09/teaching-911-attacks-prominent-history-textbooks

Jeong, Howon. (2000). *Peace and Conflict Studies: An Introduction.* London: Ashgate.

Kachun, Mitch. (2003). *Festivals of Freedom: Memory and Meaning in African-American Emancipation Celebrations, 1808–1915.* Amherst: University of Massachusetts Press.

Khan, Muaaz. "Marvel's newest hero is a Muslim girl. Entertainment industry take note." *The Guardian.* Accessed Nov. 2013 online at http://www.theguardian.com/commentisfree/2013/nov/13/marvel-muslim-comic-book-hero

Khubova, Daria, Andrei Ivankiev, and Tonia Sharova "After Glasnost. (2005). "Oral History in the Soviet Union," in Memory and Totalitarianism, ed. Luisa Passerini. . . . *Memory and Totalitarianism.* Piscataway, NJ: Transaction Publishers.

Korostelina, Karina. (2011). "Can history heal the trauma?" in Charbonneau, Bruno and Geneviève Parent, eds. *Peacebuilding, Memory and Reconciliation: Bridging Top-Down and Bottom-up Approaches.* London: Routledge.

Lantieri, Linda and Janet Patti. (1996). *Waging Peace in Our Schools.* Boston: Beacon Press.

Lederach, John Paul. (2005). *The Moral Imagination: The Art and Soul of Building Peace.* Oxford: Oxford University Press.

Mack, John. (1971). "Nationalism and the Self." *Psychohistory Review,* 2(2–3/ Spring 1985): 47–69.

Maddow, Rachel. (2012). *Drift: The Unmooring of American Military Power.* New York: Crown Publishers.

Malott, Curry Stephenson and Porfilio, Bradley. (2011). *Critical Pedagogy in the 21st Century.* Charlotte, NC: Information Age.

McLaren, Peter and Joe Kincheloe. (2007). Critical Pedagogy: where are we now? NYC: Peter Lang Publishing.

McDonald, John and Louise Diamond. (1996). *Multi-Track Diplomacy: a Systems Approach to Peace.* West Hartford, CT: Kumarian Press.

McGlynn, Claire, et al., eds. (2009). *Peace Education in Conflict and Post-Conflict Societies.* New York: Palgrave Macmillan.

Miall, Hugh, Oliver Ramsbotham and Tom Woodhouse. (2011). *Contemporary Conflict Resolution.* 3rd Edition. Cambridge: Polity Press.

Montessori, Maria. 1949. *Education and Peace.* Trans. Helen R. Lane. Chicago: Henry Regnery Publishing.

Morgan, Matthew, ed. (2009). *The Day that Changed Everything? The Impact of 9/11 on Psychology and Education.* New York: Palgrave Macmillan.

Morton, Julie. (2009). "Reading and Writing Peace: the core skills of conflict transformation." In Ndura and Amster, eds. *Building Cultures of Peace: transdisciplinary voices of hope and action.* Newcastle upon Tyne: Cambridge Scholars Publishing.

Müller-Fahrenholz, Geiko. (2006). *America's Battle for God: A European Christian Looks at Civil Religion.* Grand Rapids, MI. Willliam B. Eerdmans Publishing Co.

Mueller, John and Mark G. Stewart. (Summer 2012.) "The Terrorism Delusion: America's Overwrought Response to September 11." *International Security.* Vol 37, No. 1. pp. 81–110.

## References   131

"Muslim Western Tensions Persist". Pew Global. Accessed online Oct 2013 at http://www.pewglobal.org/2011/07/21/muslim-western-tensions-persist/

Ndura, Elavie (2009). "The role of education in peace-building in the Africa Great Lakes region: educators' perspectives." *Journal of Peace Education*, 6(1): 37–49.

Olick, Jeffery K, et al., eds. (2011). *The Collective Memory Reader*. Oxford: Oxford University Press.

Passerini, Luisa, ed. (2005). *Memory and Totalitarianism*. Piscataway, NJ: Transaction Publishers.

Priest, Dana and William Arkin. "A Hidden World, Growing Beyond Control." *A Washington Post Investigation*. Online at http://projects.washingtonpost.com/top-secret-america/articles/a-hidden-world-growing-beyond-control/

Priest, Dana and William Arkin. (2011). "Top Secret America: The Rise of the New American Security State." New York: Back Bay Books.

Pyszcznsi, Thomas A., Sheldon Solomon, and Jeff Greenberg. (2003). *In the Wake of 9/11: The Psychology of Terror*. Washington DC: American Psychological Association.

Ramsbotham, Oliver, Tom Woodhouse and Hugh Miall. (2011). *Contemporary Conflict Resolution*. 3rd Edition. Cambridge, UK: Polity Press.

Ravitch, Diane. (2013). *Reign of Error: the hoax of the privatization movement and the danger to American's public schools*. NYC: Alfred A Knopf.

Roberts, Brian. (2002). *Biographical Research*. NY: Open University Press.

Romanowski, Michael H. (2009). "Excluding Ethical Issues from U.S. History Textbooks: 9/11 and the War on Terror." *American Secondary Education*, 37(2): 26–48.

Rubenstein, Rich. (2008). "Institutions", Cheldelin, et al, eds. *Conflict*, 2nd ed. London: Continuum Press.

Rubenstein, Rich. (2010). *Reasons to Kill*. New York: Bloomsbury.

Scahill, Jeremey. (2013). *Dirty Wars*. New York: Nation Books.

Sentana, Ezechiel. (2009). *Peacebuilding in Post-Genocide Rwanda: the role of cooperatives in the restoration of interpersonal relationships*. Dissertation. University of Gothenburg.

Sherif, Muzafer. (1958). "Superordienate Goals in the Reduction of Intergroup Conflict." *American Journal of Sociology*, 63: 4. http://www.owlnet.rice.edu/~ajv2/courses/12c_psyc438001/Sherif%20(1958).pdf

Silberstein, Sandra. (2002). *War of Words: Language, Politics and 9/11*. London: Routledge.

Simon, Roger. (1991). *Gramsci's Political Thought*. London: Lawrence and Wishart.

Schirch, Lisa. (2005). *The Little Book of Strategic Peacebuilding*. Intercourse, PA: Good Books

Sturken, Marita. (1997). *Tangled Memories: The Vietnam War, the AIDS Epidemic and the Politics of Remembering*. BerkeleyUniversity of California Press.

Talbott, Strobe and Nayan Chanda. (2001). *The Age of Terror: America and the World after Sept 11*. New York: Basic Books.

Taylor, Jennifer F. (2002). "Facilitating Difficult Discussions: Processing the September 11 Attacks in Undergraduate Classrooms." *Analyses of Social Issues and Public Policy*, 2(1): 143–150.

Thoms, Annie. (2002). *With Their Eyes: Sept. 11—The View from a High School at Ground Zero*. New York: HarperCollins.

Tidwell, Alan C. (2001). *Conflict Resolved?* London: Pinter Publishers.

Torres, Lisa. (2011). "Integrating 9/11 throughout the Study of American History and Beyond." *The Social Studies*, 102(4): 158–159.

Towns, Eleni. (2011). "The 9/11 Generation." *Center for American Progress*. Available online at: http://www.americanprogress.org/issues/religion/news/2011/09/08/10363/the-911-generation/

132  *References*

Troutman, Stephanie. "Considering curriculum in post-9/11 cultural contexts: The "Story of Movies" and the politicization of the American citizen." The Pennsylvania State University, 2011. 3483746.

Volkan, Vamik. (1998). *Bloodlines: from Ethnic Pride to Ethnic Terrorism*. Boulder, CO: Westview Press.

———(2002). "Sept 11 and Societal Regression." *Group Analysis*, 35: 456.

———(2005). "Large Group Identity and Chosen Trauma". *Psychoanalysis Down Under*, 6. Online at http://www.psychoanalysisdownunder.com.au/downunder/backissues/6/427/large_group_vv

Volkan, Vamik, Demitrios A. Julius, Joseph V. Montiville, eds. (1990). *The Psychodynamics of International Relationships: vol 1*. Washington DC: Lexington.

Waterson, Robert A. and Matt Rickey. (2011). "9/11: Maintaining Relevance for the Classroom Student." *The Social Studies*, 102(4): 167–172.

Weber, Max. The Theory of Social and Economic Organization. Translated by A.M. Henderson and Talcott Parsons. London: Collier Macmillan Publishers, 1947.

Westheimer, Joel. (2007). *Pledging Allegiance: The Politics of Patriotism in America's Schools*. New York: Teacher's College Press.

Winslade J. and G.D. Monk. (2008). *Practicing Narrative Mediation: Loosening the Grip of Conflict*. San Francisco: Jossey-Bass.

Zembylas, Michalanos. (2008). *The Politics of Trauma in Education*. New York: Palgrave Macmillan.

Zingone, Joe. (2011). "9/11: Reflections, Memories, and Questions". *The Social Studies*, 102(4): 164–166.

Zinn, Howard (with Donaldo Macedo). (2005). *On Democratic Education*. Boulder, CO: Paradigm Publishers.

# Index

**A**

Afghanistan 4, 9, 14–15, 18, 46, 76, 86–87, 92–94, 101, 106, 114
Al Qaeda 23–25, 51, 54, 62, 98
Anderson, Benedict 45, 54
Arendt, Hannah 15, 108, 110

**B**

Bajaj, Monisha 29, 31, 45, 116
Beckerman, Zvi 31–36, 40, 45, 116
Boulding, Elise 30
Bullying 29, 38, 41, 49, 61–62, 98, 111
Burton, John 19
Bush, George W. 3, 22, 25–26, 64, 74, 77, 82

**C**

CAIR Council on American Islamic Relations 16
Chomsky, Noam 112
Chosen trauma 7–17, 19–25, 28–29, 31, 33–37, 39, 41, 43, 45–46, 59, 71, 77, 79, 83, 109, 112
Cobb, Sarah 18, 31, 33–34, 94, 96, 108–109, 113–115, 117
Cold War 63, 92, 101, 114
Critical emotional praxis 36–38

**D**

Dangerous memories 36–37
Drones 88
drone strikes 14, 18, 26, 38, 46

**F**

Foucault, Michel 5, 112
Freire, Paolo 29, 38–40, 66, 116
Futures visioning 29–30

**G**

Galtung, Johan 33
Genocide 7, 9, 16, 19, 29, 31, 38, 71, 86, 110

Giroux, Henry 45, 57, 102

**H**

Holocaust 13, 16, 20, 70–71, 73, 118
human rights 27, 29, 31, 41, 108, 112

**I**

Interdisciplinary curriculum 42, 48, 57, 63, 116
Internet, role of 50, 52, 79, 87, 97
Iraq 4, 9, 14–15, 18, 22, 26, 46, 53, 66–68, 76, 79, 81, 85–87, 92–93, 106, 113

**J**

Jim Crow 20

**L**

Lederach, JP 18, 32–35

**M**

Manufacture of consent 112
Media, role of 1, 2, 6, 7, 8, 9, 12–13, 15–16, 21–22, 24, 27, 31, 38, 45, 52, 61, 63, 66, 69, 78, 85–87, 90–93, 95–96, 98, 110, 114–116, 118
Montessori, Maria 38–40, 66, 111, 116

**N**

natality 110

**O**

Obama, President Barak 14, 22, 24, 28, 98
Oral histories 29–30, 75, 90–91, 96, 114

**P**

Pakistan 14, 46, 61–62, 65, 83

134  *Index*

**R**
Ravitch, Diane 57, 105–106, 114
Rhee, Michelle 104
Russia 4, 33
Rwanda 9, 16, 19, 72, 86, 110

**S**
School violence 29, 38, 41, 62
Slavery 13
Somalia 24, 63 14, 46
Soviet Union 63
Standardized testing 104, 118
Systemic conflict resolution 33
Surveillance 13, 50, 79, 105–106, 119

**T**
Trans-generational transmission 8

Transgenerational transmission 7, 9, 11, 12, 19
Torture 16, 22–23, 44, 46, 66–67, 79, 85, 87, 93, 119
Terror management theory 24

**V**
Volkan, Vamik 5, 7–10, 12, 14, 19–22, 35, 79

**Y**
Yemen 14, 46

**Z**
Zembylas, Michalanos 13, 17, 31- 36, 40, 45, 116, 119
Zinn, Howard 30, 38, 90, 96, 111, 117

An environmentally friendly book printed and bound in England by www.printondemand-worldwide.com

This book is made entirely of sustainable materials; FSC paper for the cover and PEFC paper for the text pages.

#0052 - 010615 - C0 - 229/152/8 [10] - CB - 9780415742016